The Tactful Texan:

A BIOGRAPHY OF
GOVERNOR WILL HOBBY

The

Tactful Texan:

A BIOGRAPHY OF
GOVERNOR WILL HOBBY

by James A. Clark

with Weldon Hart

RANDOM HOUSE · *NEW YORK*

To Jessica and Bill

look into his life, you will find more than you can write about him."

Three of Governor's good friends did most of the research on the book. Merita Mills of the *Beaumont Enterprise* researched Governor's Beaumont days. One of the grandest men in Texas journalism, Edmunds Travis, who lived through the Hobby administrations as an unofficial advisor and has been with him on the *Post* and in other ventures since, did the Austin research. He went deep into the state files and archives and got from Raymond Brooks, Governor's secretary (and before that a reporter for him), much of the behind-the-scenes information. The other researcher was Alice Kilman, wife of Ed Kilman, editor of the *Post* editorial page. Mrs. Kilman did the Houston and the *Post* research.

After the manuscript was written, it was carefully studied, and much of it revised, by Weldon Hart, a former Austin newspaperman and long-time associate and advisor of some of Texas' leading statesmen.

This book probably is not objective. It is hard for one who knows him to be objective about Will Hobby.

JAMES A. CLARK

CONTENTS

The Tactful Texan:

A BIOGRAPHY OF
GOVERNOR WILL HOBBY

1

Unsought Honor

THE HIGH-DOMED granite capitol of Texas, sprawling across its gentle hill at the head of Congress Avenue in Austin, looked somnolent and imperturbable in the early autumn sun. Inside, as the afternoon of September 25, 1917, wore on, tension fairly crackled through the vaulted corridors.

In the senate chamber, with its lofty, ornate, glass ceiling, the members solemnly prepared a formal judgment, removing from office the governor of Texas. They had already convicted him on ten articles of impeachment.

Before they were through, a red-faced, proud, defiant man strode into the secretary of state's office downstairs and turned in his resignation. In spite of the senate's action, ex-Governor James Edward Ferguson announced, he would be a candidate for a third term.

Nearby, in a modest side office of the executive suite, a quiet little Deep East Texan sat and meditated upon a fate that brought him exalted position he had not sought, in a manner he would never have chosen.

William Pettus Hobby, thirty-nine years of age, from the fringe of the Big Thicket in Polk County via the newspaper shops of Houston and Beaumont, was the new governor of Texas.

As lieutenant governor, elected and re-elected by the people, it was his constitutional duty to fill the breach. He did not flinch from the prospect, but he had to admit it was a somber one.

It was a day of considerable travail for Texas and the other states. The country was six months deep into a world war that was growing daily in scope and ferocity. Texas, with the rest of the states, was bustling with war work and war talk. There were reports of German submarines off Galveston, rumors of German intrigues on the Mexican border, the sight of army camps and airfields burgeoning—Camp MacArthur, Camp Logan, Camp Travis, Camp Bowie, Leon Springs, Hicks Field, Call Field, Kelly Field—and Texans everywhere were flexing muscles, shouldering Springfields, opening wallets in response to the urgent admonition, "Do Your Bit."

But the emergencies of wartime were not all that awaited Governor Will Hobby.

The state was in the second year of a devastating drought, which threatened its primarily agricultural economy. And an army of pink bollworms was relentlessly chewing its way through the thirsty Texas cotton fields, where farmers—big-scale planters and one-mule sharecroppers alike—hopefully cultivated their principal money crop.

Texans, already sharply divided over prohibition, now had the "Ferguson question" to accent their political partition. State agencies were in a condition approaching paralysis as a result of the bitter infighting on Capitol Hill. Important legislative programs had gone begging while the representatives and senators charged and defended Jim Ferguson, the dynamic Bell County banker-lawyer with a fine native flair for inspiring fierce loyalties . . . and hatreds.

Will Hobby had generally supported the campaigns and legislative programs of Jim Ferguson. He had taken no part in the impeachment procedures, although many of his friends had fought Ferguson. The Ferguson people had little reason to resent him, personally. But these were not reasonable days. The faithful would have resented anyone who occupied the chair rightfully belonging (they felt) to their beloved "Farmer Jim."'

And so it was that on a sweltering, melodramatic September afternoon, Governor Hobby found himself looking into the whites of the eyes of Ferguson appointees in nearly every important state post. He knew they could not be considered friendly to his administration.

War, drought, bollworms, hostile officials—these were the dubious inheritance of William Pettus Hobby, twenty-seventh governor of Texas.

When Captain and Mrs. Edwin Hobby celebrated the birth of a son on March 26, 1878, in Moscow, Texas, possibly they dreamed—in the fond manner of proud parents—that the fine little fellow might be destined for political fame: state senator, perhaps, as his father had been for three terms after he doffed his ragged gray Confederate uniform; or district judge, in which important office the staunch captain himself was destined to serve. Edwin Hobby was a native of Florida and an ante-bellum immigrant to Texas by way of Georgia. He was an excellent constitutional lawyer whose forte was land law, a subject upon which he wrote a book that became the basic work in Texas. His brother Alfred was a noted Texas poet and writer who had also been a settler, soldier and legislator. Will's mother, Eudora Adeline Pettus, was a daughter of old Virginia.

Surely there was political blood in Will Hobby's veins, and he showed an early interest in politics and government. His father's fireside commentaries on the jury trials in his courtroom; the brilliant arguments of the lawyers; the human interest stories, humorous and tragic, which always thrive among the sober legalities of a courthouse; and the difficult decisions he had to make—all these intrigued the boy.

But there were other important things to do in Moscow, and later in Houston and Beaumont, and somehow Will Hobby seemed to be forever choosing paths that led away from political glory for himself. They were interesting trails, too—like those probing into the Big Thicket, that two-million-acre primeval jungle which lay to the southeast of Moscow.

Captain Hobby and his four sons—Edwin, Paul, Alfred and Will—frequently explored the fringes of this dark domain of rolling hills and impassable marshlands. They had to be careful, for a man could get lost in the Big Thicket and never be heard from again. Its vast bulk was literally impenetrable; in early days it almost halted migration from Louisiana to the West.

It was a virgin country, where the elevations were covered with magnolia, tupelo, gum, cypress, mulberry, persimmon and a host of other trees, and the lowlands abounded in palmetto, water hyacinth, rare orchids and wild grape vines. Shrubs galore added their color and snare-like shoots to the tangle. The boys might find, in season, such delicacies as black and red haws, chinquapins, wild plums and papaws. Here flourished the dogwood, whose delicate white blossom traditionally ushers in the Texas political season. The Hobby boys might take home to Mother and the sisters, Mary and Laura Aline, some pungent bay leaves for the clothes chests, or sprigs of rich-green holly for Christmas decorations, or, in the fall, a slender spray of yaupon berries.

If it was hunting a man wanted to do, he could count on finding nearly anything he was after and probably a few things he wasn't looking for. Bear and beaver, extinct in most other areas of Texas, mingled there with bobcats, coons, possums and all the common varieties of game. Frequently, the hunters disturbed huge congregations of bright-plumed waterfowl on excursion from the Gulf of Mexico coast country.

And you might stumble upon a criminal, a deserter or some other form of human outcast. The Thicket was a sanctuary for that ilk, too.

At the northwestern edge, near Livingston, existed the remnants of Texas' last Indian tribes, the Alabamas and Coushattas. General Sam Houston, the Raven himself, set aside a portion of this great forest land as a last earthly hunting ground for his red brothers.

But Polk County, in the post-Civil War days as now, had more to offer than thickets, wild game and tame Indians. It had rich soil and vast native forests of longleaf yellow pine and hardwood timber. It was country where, according to regional spellbinders, the pine trees grew so tall they tickled the toes of the angels. Men came, of course, to slash down the great trees and turn them into lumber. Sawmills dotted the countryside, and around them grew up such colorful camp towns as Moscow, Onalaska, Kickapoo, Colita, Pluck, Soda, Camp Ruby, Leggett, Camden and Pointblank.

Young Will Hobby had barely started to school, when his father was elected district judge and the family moved to the county seat, Livingston. As he grew older, Will, still loving hills and woods, turned his attention more and more to books. His favorites were Dickens' novels, Shakespeare's plays and Macaulay's histories. The stories of Mark Twain, Bret Harte and James Fenimore Cooper excited his imagination as he read them over and over. But above all, he was fascinated by the biographies of American immortals, such as Washington, Lincoln, Lee and Jefferson.

As for Texas history, he learned much of it from sources close to the action itself—his father, his uncle and their friends, who had come to Texas when the state was very young. They gave him first-person accounts of the War Between the States. Thus whetted, his appetite for history grew into an avocation of a lifetime.

Life was good in Polk County, in a good country with good people. Then, one day in 1892, Will Hobby's idyllic life was shattered.

The blow was a fairly common one among men who hold public office: Judge Hobby failed to get re-elected. It was his first political defeat, and a crushing and unexpected reverse to a man who had given most of his life to public service. To young Will it was more than a reverse; it was a tragedy. If there had ever been a thought in his mind of a political career, that experience would have eliminated it.

Judge Hobby was more philosophical; he reminded his family that such was the fortune of politics. Anyway, he said, his old friend John Henry Kirby had been after him to go to Houston as a partner in the practice of law. The Hobbys would move to Houston.

John Henry Kirby—the name was already famous in Will Hobby's Texas, and growing in prestige throughout the state—was more of a businessman than a lawyer. He was a pioneering leader in the development of the East Texas lumbering industry. He wanted Judge Hobby's services as a land law expert.

A few weeks before Will reached his fifteenth birthday, the Hobbys boarded the Houston East and West Texas Railway for Houston. Perhaps the youngster, glum at leaving his home country and uncertain of his future in the big city, was inclined at first to take seriously the humor of local wags who called the H. E. & W. T., "Hell Either Way You Take it."

But the resilience of youth and the strange experience of bumping along on the little narrow-gauge tracks toward new adventures soon prevailed over his misgivings. He was entranced by the changing country outside the grimy car windows. The forests and rolling hills of East Texas gradually vanished, and the train puffed along on the wide, flat, grassy prairies of the coastal plains.

It was after dark when the Hobbys arrived at the old H. E. & W. T. depot in Houston's turbulent Fifth Ward. Long lines of hacks and drays waited in line. The electric lights in the waiting rooms were bright almost beyond belief. Riding in a hack to the Tremont Hotel, he marveled at the wide, dusty streets and how they crossed each other at regular intervals all the way. He heard his father say that more than 50,000 people lived in Houston. Along the street men were hawking hot tamales and popcorn. Swarms of people were still up, walking and laughing and talking. Lights were still on everywhere. It was nothing like Moscow or Livingston.

Will began to feel that it was a good thing, after all, that his father had lost the election and that Mr. Kirby had sent for him to come to Houston.

Soon the Hobbys were settled in a new home on the South Side, on McKinney Avenue. It was Will's first year in high school. He attended classes in a huge old brick building, while a new and modern central high school was going up a little farther away from the growing business district, but even the temporary location seemed like a castle compared to the little schoolhouse in Livingston.

Of all the exciting attractions of Houston, the greatest was right next door to the temporary school building on Congress Avenue. Here the *Houston Post* was edited and printed, and the roaring presses attracted him like a magnet. In the morning he stopped to watch the newspapers come tumbling off the line, like big white chips down a millrace. He heard the newsboys shouting the headlines as they grabbed armloads of papers and streamed out of the alley. When school was out, he sauntered along in front of the entrance to see and sometimes even speak to the reporters and editors.

Each day Will became more certain that this was the business for him. Here were excitement, glamour, romance, opportunity.

One memorable day Governor Jim Hogg came to town for the Dick Dowling Confederate Ball. This warm, friendly, tremendous man visited the newspaper plant, and Will spoke to him as he came out. Gentleman Jim Corbett, the world's heavyweight boxing champion, once visited his classroom with the *Post* sports reporter. But the greatest thrill of all came the day Will followed one of his reporter friends down to the Grand Central Station.

"Come along, kid," the reporter had said. "There's something down at the depot I think you'll want to see."

It was a special barred railroad car filled with federal prisoners being transferred from the West to the Atlanta Penitentiary. There, in the center of the car, was Geronimo, the mighty Apache war chief. Will listened while the reporter talked to the old brave and took notes as Geronimo grunted and grimaced and fanned the air with great, deliberate gestures of indignation.

Such a world was too entrancing for Will Hobby to live in only before and after school. He was sixteen years old and already had more formal education than the average boy of that era. One night he broke the news to his father and mother: Mr. G. J. Palmer, business manager of the *Post*, had offered him a job in the circulation department for eight dollars a week. He wanted to take it.

Judge and Mrs. Hobby argued the advantages of continuing his education, but Will had arguments of his own: the judge was in failing health and no longer able to work long hours at the office; the eight dollars a week would enable Will to buy his own clothing, help a little with the grocery bills, and allow him to be a man on his own. It was finally agreed that he could stay out of school until the following September. Perhaps by then, thought his parents, times would be better and the newspaper world would have lost some of its fascination.

Will Hobby gathered up his textbooks, said good-by to his teachers and friends—reminding them, however, that he would still be next door at the *Houston Post*—and left without the slightest intention of ever darkening another schoolhouse door.

2

Newsman by Choice

IT WAS Texas Independence Day, March 2, 1895. In Houston only the newspaper offices and the drug stores kept shop. That morning the *Post* carried the complete text of William Jennings Bryan's "Silver Manifesto," antecedent of his famous "Cross of Gold" speech at the 1896 Democratic Convention. From Austin, the *Post* correspondent was chiding the Texas legislators who were on a junket to Monterrey after "doing as little as any legislature could possibly do in a fifty-six-day session." A wire story noted that the Minnesota state legislature had passed a resolution proclaiming the adjournment of Congress as "an hour of deliverance."

Grover Cleveland was President of the United States and Charles A. Culberson was the new governor of Texas, having succeeded the great James Stephen Hogg. Houston was one of Texas' three largest cities and almost doubling in population every ten years.

Will Hobby, on his first day as a newspaperman, thought it was a wonderful world.

Mr. Palmer showed him to his place in the mail room. It was not an elaborate location; as a matter of fact, it was the merest cubbyhole, but young Hobby found it adequate. His job was to keep the out-of-town circulation lists in order and to answer any complaints concerning them.

The *Post* editorial room bulged with talent. Nat Floyd, a

11

fine writer; Jim Quarles, an aggressive reporter; William Sydney Porter, a columnist with a deft, original touch; Marcellus E. Foster, a little, red-faced man with a towering shock of curly black hair and a touch of genius at his finger tips— these were some of the star performers of the daily journalistic show ringmastered by the redoubtable Rienzi Melville Johnston, editor-in-chief and one of the South's leading editors and political analysts.

Rienzi Johnston was a Confederate veteran who had started his military career at the ripe age of twelve, as a drummer boy in the Confederate Army. At fourteen he had been accepted for enlistment in the fighting ranks. Before Appomattox his comrades had elected him a lieutenant. The passing years brought him the inevitable promotion accorded nearly all surviving Confederates, and he was Colonel Johnston to one and all.

Johnston joined the *Post* in 1885 as Austin correspondent, coming from the *Austin Statesman.* That was the year Julius Lewis Watson revived the *Post,* a five-year-old sheet started by Gail Borden Johnson, from an economic sinking spell. Watson, Johnston and the *Post* prospered together, so that when Will Hobby came on the scene a decade later he was joining a successful and respected newspaper.

From the first, Hobby's principal interest was in the editorial room, where the news was written and edited and where glamorous young demigods of the editorial staff turned out columns and poems that made readers laugh and cry. Will's favorite, however, was Sydney Porter.

Porter was in his early thirties, an attractive fellow with a blond mustache and light, wavy hair. He was quiet and reserved, often to the point of moroseness. But he took a fancy to young Hobby, and the two frequently sat together in Porter's office after he put the finishing touches on his column, "Postscripts."

Mr. Porter, as Will called him, was a fascinating storyteller. Frequently the boy would run out for sandwiches and coffee and have lunch with Sydney Porter, in the hope of hearing more wonderful stories. This promising writer had quit school even earlier than Will. He had been a drug clerk, a ranch hand, a clerk in the state land office, a bank teller, a magazine editor. Writing was obviously the career for which he was suited.

Little more than a year after Hobby went to work, after the *Post* moved to its new plant on the northeast corner of Franklin and Fannin Streets, he was promoted to cashier. A man came into the business office one day looking for Sydney Porter. Hobby proudly directed the stranger to his favorite's office.

The next day he learned that the visitor had been an officer from Austin with a summons for Porter. The ex-bank teller had been charged with embezzlement. Porter left immediately by train for Austin. It was said later that he changed from a westbound to an eastbound train at Hempstead, fifty miles from Houston, and headed for New Orleans. From there he had taken a banana boat to Honduras.

The depressing story reached a climax for Will Hobby about a year later when he heard that Sydney Porter had returned to Austin to be with his seriously ill wife, Athol, had been arrested and convicted on the embezzlement charge and sent to the federal penitentiary at Columbus, Ohio. After serving his time, Porter went to New York, where until his death in 1910 he earned increasing fame as a writer of short stories. The world remembers him as O. Henry.

Will Hobby remembers him as a talented newspaperman who took time to be kind to a spindly-legged East Texas boy from the mail room.

In 1897, after Hobby had moved on to a new job in the advertising department, Publisher J. L. Watson died. He left his *Post* stock to his son, Roy Garrett Watson, who was only five years old. The stock was left in trust until the lad should reach his twenty-fifth birthday, and Colonel Rienzi Johnston, Henry F. MacGregor and G. J. Palmer—the man who gave Will Hobby his first job—were designated as trustees.

Colonel Johnston became president, as well as editor-in-chief, of the *Post*. MacGregor, who never entered into the active management of the paper, was a New Englander, as staunchly Republican politically as Johnston was Democratic.

MacGregor was a businessman and banker of high standing in Houston, and Johnston liked and respected him, but the doughty Colonel gave no quarter when it came to politics. The *Post* continued to be anti-Republican and pro-Democratic.

Rienzi Johnston took a genuine interest in young Will Hobby. The Colonel was a good friend of John Henry Kirby, law partner of Will's father. He knew the boy had inherited a good political background, and Johnston was always as much interested in politics as he was in newspapering. He was impressed when Will borrowed $1,000 to buy ten shares of *Post* stock in April, 1900.

In that same year, Will Hobby, just turned twenty-one, habitually quiet and almost laconic, further interested Colonel Johnston by making his first political speech. The occasion was the Harris County Democratic Convention. The *Houston Herald,* an opposition afternoon newspaper run by a colorful editor named Bill Bailey, had successfully backed the candidacy of Sam Brashear for mayor. The *Post* had backed the loser, John T. Browne.

A resolution was offered condemning the *Post*. John T. Browne arose to defend the morning paper and moved that the resolution be tabled. At this stage young Hobby made his political debut.

He stood up to second Browne's motion and, somewhat prophetically, made a strong plea for party harmony. Colonel Johnston watched the proceedings with considerable interest. The Colonel was not much of a man for harmony himself, but he was intrigued by the political precocity of his young colleague.

The next few months brought two unforgettable stories to the *Post's* doorstep. In September, 1900, the Galveston storm, one of the great catastrophies of history, struck savagely at the thriving rival city fifty miles south of Houston. Galveston was almost literally wiped off the face of the earth by a tremendous hurricane and some 6,000 of its citizens perished. Houston, badly flooded but not permanently damaged, became a haven for refugees from Galveston and, incidentally, for much of Galveston's business and industry.

Four months later it seemed that Nature sought to make amends to Southeast Texas for its fury at Galveston. The selected site was a little mound of earth just south of Beaumont, eighty miles east of Houston—Spindletop! There the famous Lucas gusher came in flowing 100,000 barrels of oil a day, to open a new age for the world at large and a vast industrial future for the country along the great Gulf Coast Bend.

Beaumont was a small sawmill town whose facilities for hospitality were strained even when a medicine show came to town. Houston benefited from the overflow. Business boomed overnight, and the *Post* boomed with it. Advertisements of wildcat oil companies doubled and redoubled the size of the paper.

Marcellus E. Foster called Will Hobby into his office one day and said he had a terrific story in the making. He needed a complete biography of John Henry Kirby.

That was an assignment Will could tackle with real enthusiasm. Kirby, of course, had been a Hobby family friend for many years. A colorful and rising figure in the business scene, his shadow was beginning to loom even past Texas borders. He was a Piney Woods boy taken barefoot out of the brush by Bronson Cooper, now the congressman from the Beaumont district, and sent to college, where he earned a law degree in amazingly fast time.

John Henry Kirby's genius for organization had resulted in the formation of one of the leading lumber companies of the South. Now he was on the verge of making a $30,000,000 deal which would include the formation of the Houston Oil Company as the most richly capitalized company of the whole fantastic Spindletop boom.

Will Hobby did a magnificent job for Marcellus Foster on the Kirby biography. The story brought Foster's promotion to managing editor . . . and a headful of ideas to young Hobby.

Foster had hardly warmed his managing editor's chair when Hobby approached him and said, "Mr. Foster, I want to be a reporter."

Foster was delighted. He was seeking someone to take over the business and markets coverage that he had developed. Will had shown an aptitude for writing, and his experience in the business end of the paper was a further qualification. The job was his, Foster said, at $22.50 a week.

It was a great day for Will Hobby, in August of 1901, when he first walked into the editorial room as a full-fledged reporter who belonged there and not merely as a hanger-on from another department. The other staff members welcomed him in his new status; he had always shown more interest in their work than in the business office, anyway. The old-time reporters warned him he was making a mistake. But Hobby just grinned—and so did they.

As collector and writer of business and market news, Hobby hit the *Post's* editorial staff at a propitious time. He covered the fabulous development of the Spindletop oil field where, in addition to Houston Oil, future corporate giants like Gulf Oil and Texas Company were being formed. The pioneers of that early oil era, such as J. S. Cullinan, Jim Hogg, Howard Hughes, Walter Sharp and dozens of others, made their homes in Houston and commuted to Beaumont on the Southern Pacific. The Great Southwest was beginning to industrialize, and Houston was the hub of activity.

The year 1902 brought big stories from around the world: the coronation of Edward VII; the eruption of Mount Pelée, on Martinique, with its 20,000 victims; the death of Zola; and, nearer home, the sensational Spindletop oil fires; and the election of O. T. Holt as mayor of Houston on a reform ticket backed by John Henry Kirby, Rienzi Johnston and the *Houston Post*.

Will Hobby continued his modest political advances at the county Democratic convention when he was named a member of the Platform Committee and elected a delegate to the state convention at Galveston. The *Post* supported Tom Ball for Congress, commending him especially for obtaining a million-dollar appropriation for the Buffalo Bayou channel that eventually was to make Houston a great inland seaport. Guided by Rienzi Johnston, the *Post* continued to speak out against women's suffrage and prohibition.

Midyear brought a significant change to the Houston newspaper situation, and to Will Hobby. Marcellus Foster, the astute managing editor of the *Post,* realized an ambition that most editors cherish futilely: he started his own newspaper.

Foster had made a modest fortune in oil speculations at Spindletop and he took it all into his new venture. He bought out Bill Bailey's troublesome but financially anemic *Herald* and combined it with his new paper, which he called the *Houston Chronicle.*

Clarence Owsley succeeded Foster as managing editor of the *Post,* and Will Hobby moved up to city editor. A few months later Owsley resigned to take another job. No new managing editor was appointed, Colonel Johnston being preoccupied with political affairs at the moment. Will Hobby, in effect, appointed himself managing editor. He moved quietly into the vacuum and received the full co-operation of the staff despite his lack of formal portfolio.

3

Two Stories High

THE YEAR 1904 was another national election year. Henry MacGregor, the *Post's* lone Republican trustee, became his party's candidate for Congress as well as a state executive committeeman. The *Post* continued to boost Democrats, as always, and to oppose Republicans—including Mr. MacGregor. Mr. MacGregor was an understanding man. He and Colonel Rienzi Johnston continued on excellent personal and business terms.

Also in 1904, Will Hobby's growing interest in politics led him into his first experience in political organization work. With the help of two friends, Chester Bryan and J. B. Marmion, he organized what was probably the first Young Democrats club in the country. They called it the Young Men's Democratic Club (there being no women voters then) and elected Hobby the first president. The senior group, the State Democratic Executive Committee, took a serious interest in the Hobby-led effort to enlist young men into the party.

Recognition came to Will Hobby for his party services. He went to the 1904 Democratic state convention as chairman of the delegation from the Sixteenth Congressional District. Frank Andrews, an eminent Houston lawyer, was elected chairman of the State Democratic Executive Committee. He promptly promoted Hobby into his first official party position —secretary to the State Committee.

It was a banner political year for the *Post*. Rienzi Johnston was re-elected Democratic national committeeman, a position he had won in 1902. John Henry Kirby was permanent chairman of the state convention. The *Post* went down the line for the illustrious, colorful and controversial Joseph Weldon Bailey for renomination as United States Senator, and for John M. Pinckney for Congress (against the *Post's* own Henry F. MacGregor). They were winners, but the *Post's* Democratic candidate for President, Alton B. Parker, was no match in the general election for Theodore Roosevelt.

Will Hobby continued to act as managing editor, without either recognition or interference from Colonel Johnston. That year the *Post* acquired a new editor. It was a fortunate strike for both.

George McClelland Bailey was a New Englander by birth and English-Welsh by ancestry. Like many outstanding newspapermen of the day, he lacked formal education. He had left school at the age of fourteen and learned the trade as a printer's devil and as a journeyman reporter in North Carolina and Texas. He came to the *Post* from a Washington assignment with the *Galveston-Dallas News*.

The *Post* had already harbored some notable editors. One was William Cowper Brann, stormy petrel of Texas journalism in the eighteen-nineties, who left the *Post* and launched his famous publication *The Iconoclast* the year before Will Hobby came to Houston. Brann's highly personal journalism inevitably ended in a shooting, on a Waco street in 1898, in which both he and a man who had been antagonized by his pen were killed. Then there was the formidable Rienzi Johnston, still very much alive and kicking but more occupied with political than with journalistic crises much of the time. There were others, but in George Bailey they had a successor worthy of their example.

A brilliant writer, Bailey confined himself to editorial comments and the direction of the paper's editorial policy, leaving to Will Hobby the various problems of newsroom administration. Hobby relished every Bailey sentence. Bailey was a pungent paragrapher, a forerunner of the modern columnist. His subjects ranged from "heavenly Houston," and its inimitable red-headed widows, to the unparalleled excellence of Walker County sausages and Waller County melons, with an occasional dig at a particularly annoying and inquisitive subscriber in Wharton. He paid appropriate tribute to the "noble Democrats" and made Henry MacGregor flinch with his comments on "depraved Republicans"—all tongue-in-cheek "Early Morning Observations," which alternated with "Paragraphorisms." The great Kentucky editor-politician, "Marse Henry" Watterson, was his friend and admirer.

While George Bailey entertained and enlightened the readers with his deft wordmanship, Will Hobby kept busy in his dual role of city editor-acting managing editor. There were many duties for him of a routine nature—in plain words, a lot of hard work. Some days, however, there was livelier fare. Such a day was April 24, 1905.

That afternoon Hobby answered the telephone in the city room. A man's voice, tense with excitement, asked, "Is this the editor of the *Post?*"

Hobby assured him that it was.

"Don't tell anybody I called you, but there's been one hell of a shooting down at Hempstead. Congressman Pinckney has been killed, and at least three other men are either dead or dying. I just got the information on my wire here at the railroad dispatcher's office. I called you because I like the *Post.*" And there was a click as the caller hung up.

Will Hobby moved into high gear. First, however, he took time to check his source. He telephoned the dispatcher's office at the Southern Pacific Railroad and asked the telegraph operator if he had just called the *Post.*

"Yes, but be quiet about it or I'll get fired," the dispatcher implored.

Hobby summoned Pat Daugherty, his best reporter, and sent him off to Hempstead. Then he called Hempstead and got a confirmation and a few more details from the telephone operator. He tried to call half a dozen friends in the little town, but excitement was running too high for local citizens to answer a telephone.

The files were quickly checked for a picture and biography of Congressman John M. Pinckney. The rest of the staff was alerted to the story and urged to use every possible means of getting through to friends in Hempstead.

In a miraculously short time Pat Daugherty was on the telephone. He had the names of John M. Pinckney, his brother Thomas D. Pinckney, a Hempstead lawyer named H. M. Brown, a farmer named J. E. Mills—all dead.

Roland Brown, son of H. M. Brown, and R. E. Tompkins, the congressman's secretary, were wounded.

Soon the details were streaming in. Behind the carnage at Hempstead was the prohibition fight, which was raging throughout Texas in those days, although usually in less violent fashion. Hempstead had had a "local option" election four days earlier. Feelings ran high; one side wanted to call for Texas Rangers to maintain the peace. At a mass meeting called to consider the question a resolution was offered asking for state officers. Certain citizens took offense at this reflection on the local constabulary.

Congressman Pinckney had spoken for the resolution. Captain H. M. Brown had spoken against it. Tompkins was up supporting Pinckney's stand when Brown interrupted him by hitting him across the head with a pistol.

From that point, the *Post* duly reported, pandemonium reigned. Twenty-five or thirty shots were fired, and six men went down—four of them dead. Brown's son, Roland, was charged with the murder of Congressman Pinckney, and Tompkins was charged with the murder of Brown.

Governor Lanham sent the Rangers to Hempstead.

This bloody incident helped earn Hempstead its sobriquet of "Six-Shooter Junction." It helped Will Hobby earn new stature as a newspaper editor. He "played the story" for all it was worth. On the morning of April 25, the entire front page of the *Post* was devoted to the sensational details of the killings. Congressman Pinckney's picture and a complete biography were carried in a box. The next day's follow-up ran two columns full on page one and all of page four, with pictures of the principals and a diagram showing where the bullets hit and where the bodies fell.

The complete and dramatic handling of this story, one of the biggest of the year in Texas, won Will Hobby his permanent billet as managing editor at the age of twenty-six. His first act was to appoint Pat Daugherty to the city editorship.

Hobby continued to prove himself a born managing editor. He loved the job, and Colonel Rienzi Johnston loved the way he handled it. The *Post* continued to grow as Houston expanded under aggressive civic leadership and the smiles of economic fortune. The oil fever which had broken out at Spindletop five years before continued over the state unabated in 1906.

Political champion of the new and flourishing oil industry was Senator Joseph Weldon Bailey. This silver-tongued native of Mississippi had represented Texas in Washington since 1891, for ten years as Congressman and as United States Senator since 1901.

Already in 1906 there were rumblings of a storm gathering around Joe Bailey's handsome head. The Waters-Pierce Oil Company was back doing business in Texas, after being ousted for violating the antitrust laws. Senator Bailey had been instrumental in the return of the company, which ostensibly had purged itself of a connection with the Standard Oil Company that had caused its difficulties in the first place. Whispers went around that Joe Bailey got a $100,000 retainer fee from Waters-Pierce. His enemies claimed he had more than a friendly relationship, too, with John Henry Kirby, the oil and lumber king.

But Bailey was, unquestionably, one of the most effective representatives Texas ever had in Washington. He was the bellwether of the Texas "wets" and of the opponents of

women's suffrage. The *Post's* Colonel Rienzi Johnston wor-
shipped at his shrine.

No mistake about it; the *Houston Post*, first and last,
scandalous rumors or not, was a Joe Bailey paper. To the
Chronicle, and Editor Marcellus E. Foster, he was anathema.

Bailey had been renominated for a second term in the
United States Senate, with election pending, by the Texas
senate. This was prior to adoption of the 17th Amendment
calling for popular election of U. S. senators. Foster believed
Bailey's election could be blocked if he were exposed as a
friend of the Standard Oil "octopus." And the logical man
to expose him was the distinguished M. M. Crane, who as
attorney general had once kicked Waters-Pierce out of Texas
because it was an instrument of Standard Oil.

The announcement electrified Houston: Joe Bailey and
M. M. Crane would meet in public debate on the evening of
October 6, 1906, in the new city auditorium.

The crowd gathered early and was modestly described by
the *Post* as the most magnificent political gathering in the
history of Texas. Between five and six thousand men and a
sprinkling of women were present. The debate was to start
at eight o'clock; by seven the auditorium was packed to the
rafters.

At the last minute the rumor started and swelled: Bailey
and Crane could not agree to terms. The debate might have
to be called off.

Bailey, in a magnanimous gesture, finally acceded to every
demand of Crane's supporters, including permission for
Crane to open and close.

Will Hobby was well aware of the tremendous news value
of this "Debate of the Century" and was prepared. He had
arranged for a battery of public stenographers to work in
shifts and take down every word of the debate. Runners were
to feed the copy to "rewrite" men in the *Post* city room. All
of page one and as many as five full inside pages were held
available for the torrent of words from the two oratorical
giants.

There was little doubt in Hobby's mind as to the outcome of the debate. Joe Bailey was invincible on the stump.

The debate started in a dignified tone. Crane was brilliant, but his reception fell far short of what the *Chronicle* had expected. He accused Bailey of the Standard Oil tie-up and then charged that the Senator had taken a $225,000 retainer from John Henry Kirby. He reviewed the oil cases he had handled as attorney general, particularly the Waters-Pierce case. He soundly upbraided Bailey for the impropriety of accepting fees from interests which, in turn, sought favors from the government. He accused Bailey of selling Kirby Lumber Company bonds to the railroads.

All of Crane's venom and vigor failed to dampen the ardor of Joe Bailey's followers. They greeted Bailey with an ovation. He cleverly handled every accusation.

He had helped Waters-Pierce, he said, but only after complete assurance that the company was divorced from Standard. He refused to acknowledge the retainer from Standard, but he freely admitted that Kirby had paid him a retainer. The wealthy lumberman had needed legal advice quickly in New York; Bailey gave it to him, and Kirby agreed (said the Senator) that he got his money's worth.

As for his selling Kirby bonds to the railroads—Senator Bailey smiled—that was impossible. The lumber company had never issued any bonds.

The evening wore on, and Bailey kept speaking. It became distressfully clear to the Crane people why the Senator had agreed to let his opponent open and close the debate. They had neglected to set a time limit on the speakers.

Senator Bailey talked until midnight. After driving home his points, he virtually filibustered until the crowd dwindled away. Crane closed to an almost empty auditorium.

Bailey's vocal marathon reminded wags of a hoary Texas political story.

The candidate visiting in a small town saw a crowd gathered on the courthouse square and could not resist the temptation. He climbed into the back end of a wagon and harangued the citizens at such length that finally everyone left except one silent farmer.

"My friend, I thank you for your courtesy," the candidate said. "Now, pray tell me, what was it in my speech that held you here after all the others departed?"

To which the farmer laconically replied, "You're standing in my wagon."

But Will Hobby and his *Post* did not make light of Joe Bailey's achievement. Every uttered word of both speakers, as well as the introductions and other remarks of preliminary speakers, appeared in the *Houston Post,* along with sketches by the staff artist. Hobby had organized and directed coverage that represented one of the major feats of Texas journalism.

As Texans faced up blithely to the panic year of 1907, William Pettus Hobby had won firm recognition as a topnotch newspaper editor.

4

Challenge of Ownership

WILL HOBBY sat in his office, where he usually thought about the problems of the *Houston Post,* and thought, instead, about the problems of the *Beaumont Enterprise.*

A visitor had just left him food for considerable reflection.

The caller was a friend, Walter Joshua Crawford of Beaumont, a member of the State Democratic Executive Committee, which Hobby had lately served as secretary.

This had been Crawford's spine-tingling message: Beaumont needed Will Hobby to run—and eventually own—the *Enterprise.*

Admittedly, the *Enterprise* was in financial difficulty. The "panic" of 1907 was on, and business nearly everywhere was suffering. But it was less the general economic depression that plagued the *Enterprise* than it was the petering out of the Spindletop oil field.

Walter Crawford's proposition was clear-cut and business-like. Beaumont needed to keep its morning daily newspaper. The *Enterprise,* without an editor, was foundering; Crawford was one of five Beaumont leaders who proposed to reorganize the company and get the operation on a sound basis. None of the five knew how to run a newspaper, nor cared to learn.

They wanted Will Hobby to leave the managing editorship of the *Houston Post* and become editor, manager, half-owner and, in time, full owner of the *Enterprise.*

In addition to that, his starting salary at Beaumont would be two hundred dollars a month. That was more than he was making as managing editor of the *Post*.

Intrigued, of course, but never a man to make impulsive decisions, Hobby weighed the proposition carefully. Beaumont, the county seat of Jefferson County, had a chance to be a thriving city even without Spindletop. When the 100,000-barrel Lucas gusher came in six years earlier, it was a sleepy lumber town of 9,000 souls. At the height of the boom as many as 50,000 people were jammed into Beaumont, counting promoters, investors, gamblers and oil field workers. Now most of the transients had departed, but Beaumont remained a city of some 20,000 population.

The *Enterprise* was the first Beaumont paper to enjoy appreciable success. The rest had lasted no longer than the first due date of the mortgage on presses and type. John W. Leonard, a naturalized Australian lawyer, founded the *Enterprise* in 1880, the same year Gail Borden Johnson founded the *Houston Post*. Leonard came from Arizona, where he published the *Arizona Daily Enterprise*—whence the name of his new Texas venture, a little weekly.

Leonard had to leave Beaumont, for reasons of health, in 1882. He turned over the *Enterprise* to T. A. Lamb, his brother-in-law. Mort L. Bixler bought it in 1896 and converted it to a morning daily. Bixler's *Enterprise* had its day of financial glory during the Spindletop boom, but wilted badly under the decline to normal business conditions.

Two more blows—the advent of the afternoon *Beaumont Journal* and the pinch of the 1907 panic—compounded Bixler's economic dilemma to the point of bankruptcy.

Will Hobby, weighing his bright prospects at the *Post* against the even higher potential of a gamble at Beaumont, turned to Colonel Rienzi Johnston for advice. The good Colonel did not relish the thought of losing Hobby. But the opportunity of becoming publisher of a daily newspaper—even one that was broke—didn't come often to a young man of barely twenty-eight. Johnston thought Hobby was capable of making a go of the *Enterprise*. And, with his habit of considering political implications, he did not overlook the advantage of having a strong young Democratic friend running a daily newspaper in the nearby city of Beaumont.

Rienzi Johnston advised Hobby to go to the *Enterprise*. So did John Henry Kirby, whose timber empire swung in a great semicircle around Beaumont. Will found no one who failed to see the move as a rare opportunity.

Hobby told Walter Crawford, "I'll be there."

The new *Enterprise* company was capitalized for $50,000. The property cost $30,000, one-third of the amount to be paid down. Hobby borrowed $5,000 from A. L. Williams, Beaumont banker, and thus controlled half of the stock from the outset. His five partners put up the other half, $1,000 each. In addition to Crawford and Williams, the stockholders were P. A. Heisig, a wholesale grocer; B. Deutser, a furniture dealer, and R. A. Greer, lawyer and capitalist.

In its issue of June 11, 1907, the *Enterprise* announced that the plant, building and business of the newspaper had been purchased by a syndicate of Beaumont businessmen. Five days later came the report of a board meeting at which William P. Hobby, formerly of the *Houston Post*, had been elected editor and general manager "with full control of the publication of the paper."

Beaumont still had its morning paper; Walter Crawford and his friends had the editor they wanted. Now it was a matter of seeing how Hobby would react to his first taste of ultimate responsibility. They did not have to wait long for an indication.

Will Hobby's first editorial in the *Enterprise* sketched the general goal: building up Beaumont and the rich surrounding territory of Southeast Texas and Southwestern Louisiana. A few days later the primary target was outlined: Beaumont was the natural junction of rail and water connections in the whole area; it should become one of the most important distributing centers of the South.

Thus Hobby demonstrated from the start that his principal interests would be civic rather than political. The *Enterprise,* he wrote, would continue to be Democratic but would favor no particular candidate. He was high, for a young man, in Texas political circles—personal friend of Colonel Rienzi Johnston, John Henry Kirby, Congressman Bronson Cooper and many lesser lights of that political day. What Beaumont needed, however, was broader vision than that of partisan politics. Political influence would sometimes be helpful and necessary, he realized, but as a means to an end.

That end soon crystallized in Will Hobby's mind and in the columns of his *Beaumont Enterprise:* the newspaper was to be a champion of the deep-water channel that would make Beaumont a genuine inland seaport.

Deep water for Beaumont was not a new dream. It had been thought about and talked about down through the years, as barges and small vessels fought the narrow, crooked channel and the treacherous shallows of the Neches River, to carry lumber, cotton, sugar cane, rice and cattle to a point where they could transfer their cargoes to seagoing freighters. In 1862 armed sloops of the United States Navy had penetrated to Beaumont, and the Federals had burned the railroad depot. But Beaumont was still a mere river station compared to, say, the newer city of Port Arthur, on Sabine Lake, where the founder, Arthur E. Stilwell, had dug a twenty-five-foot channel to Sabine Pass.

Out through Sabine Pass was deep water, the Gulf of Mexico. Beaumont sorely needed a channel that could bring seagoing vessels to its doorstep. Orange, up the neighboring Sabine River, nursed similar ambitions. The dream even had an official name: the Sabine-Neches Waterway.

Congressman Bronson Cooper tried to sell Washington on the idea of a nine-foot channel to Beaumont and Orange, to form the forks of a Y, with a similar channel across shallow Sabine Lake as the trunk. In 1904 he got a $125,000 appropriation; in 1905 he raised it to $411,000. But the program had bogged down; no one was pushing it.

No one, that is, until Will Hobby came to Beaumont.

In less than a week Hobby was blasting away at discriminatory rail freight rates which, he pointed out, made it all the more imperative for Beaumont to have access to deep water. At the same time he was urging the quiescent Deep Water Committee to get on with the dredging of the Sabine-Neches Waterway. Soon the committee was calling on Congressman Cooper to find out what was holding up the dredging program. Early in July the *Enterprise* jolted city fathers into action on a project to grade the city wharf site.

Hobby rarely let an issue of the *Enterprise* come out without one of his forceful editorials about a deep-water channel, which he envisioned as a great artery pumping rich economic blood into the underdeveloped Beaumont-Orange-Port Arthur triangle. He found that Congress had already approved a twenty-five-foot canal fifteen miles long and two-hundred-feet wide to make a seaport of Newark, N. J. He said there was little difference between what Beaumont was asking and what Newark had been given. The difference, he intimated, was that Newark citizens had shown Congress the facts and figures while Beaumont citizens hadn't. He took the citizenry to task for criticizing Congressman Cooper when they had done little or nothing to help him.

This aggressive, big-city brand of newspapering proved a tonic for Beaumont business. The Chamber of Commerce and other civic organizations began to stir. Before long Will Hobby was on every important civic improvement committee in the town.

In November he was urging Beaumont citizens to take an interest in the Inland Waterways Convention at Houston, because the proposed intracoastal canal would become an integral part of Jefferson County's communication system. A month later he was paying his disrespects to Uncle Joe Cannon, the Speaker of the House, for opposing waterways programs like Beaumont's. Hobby labeled Cannon a "stand-patter" who wanted to pile up a federal surplus instead of putting the tax money back into circulation through contracts for beneficial public works.

While Will Hobby thought about and worked for the industrial future of his chosen city, his banker kept sending him disagreeable reminders of present problems. The *Enterprise* was expanding; in Hobby's first month it gained eight-hundred in circulation. But expenses still exceeded its income.

Banker Al Williams, one of Hobby's five partners, labored under the apprehension that the paper might have to go into receivership again. Hobby had to spend hours each week reassuring Williams that the *Enterprise,* given time and a diminution of the economic "panic," would surely make the grade.

Week after week Hobby had to dig to the bottom of the barrel for money to meet payrolls. Banker Williams once warned him not to write payroll checks that week; the funds were not there, and the bank wasn't going to honor any more overdrafts. Hobby wrote the checks anyway, boarded a train for New Orleans and didn't return until the middle of the following week. As he had anticipated, Williams, unable to reach him, had honored the checks.

Hobby's individual depression was of short duration. In a few weeks the tide began to turn. It soon became apparent that the *Enterprise* had weathered the economic storm of 1907.

Hobby started 1908 with another drive, this time one to make Beaumont a sub-port of entry. On January 23 he wrote that it was possible for Beaumont to become the leading port of the Southwest, even larger than Galveston or Houston.

Two days later, somewhat symbolically, the last cut was made in the Sabine-Neches canal and the waters of the two rivers were joined with the Gulf of Mexico.

On January 29, 1908, Will Hobby proudly served as a member of a reception committee to greet the revenue cutter *Windom*—the city's first ocean-going visitor—when it tied up at the foot of Main Street. The *Enterprise* proclaimed it "the greatest water event in the history of Beaumont."

The first important commercial use of the new waterway

came in February when the seagoing tugboat *Higgins,* named for the Pattillo Higgins whose explorations led to the Spindletop oil bonanza, docked at Beaumont. In April another Spindletop pioneer, Captain W. C. Tyrrell, purchased the steamship *Nicaragua.* The *Enterprise* called for a celebration and a full cargo for the *Nicaragua,* when it roared into port with the honor of being Beaumont's first ocean steamer.

Editor Hobby was after the City Council to build a new dock at the foot of Main Street. Evidently he was not going to be satisfied with the minor triumph of a mere nine-foot channel down the Neches. The future amply bore out that indication.

Meanwhile Hobby celebrated the progress both of Beaumont as a seaport and of the *Enterprise* as a newspaper with a forty-eight-page "Deep Water-Immigration" special edition. Coming out on May 5, the fat and fact-filled issue marked a new journalistic milestone for Beaumont. Of more immediate interest to the publisher, it also marked the end of the *Enterprise's* financial crisis. Hobby promptly bought out two of his five partners. Williams and Greer. That move gave him 70 percent of *Enterprise* stock.

Beaumonters settled back to enjoy the fruits of their labors, which were bringing a new economic force into the life of the city. On the anniversary of Will Hobby's arrival, they got another jolt.

The nine-foot channel was well and good, the *Enterprise* noted; it was a step in the right direction. But what Beaumont really needed, and had to have, was a twenty-five-foot channel.

Hobby and the *Enterprise* were off again, this time on a crusade to make Beaumont a true deep-water port.

5

In Spindletop's Wake

As BEAUMONT MOVED into the second and vital phase of its port improvement program, Will Hobby saw two necessities: to keep the citizens interested, and to get the money necessary for the project. The *Enterprise* would take care of the former; the latter would require the concerted efforts of many people.

At first the prospect was roseate. Public complacency, which Hobby feared might follow completion of the nine-foot channel, was never allowed to develop. Most Beaumont businessmen quickly grasped the larger vision; a real deep-water port would enhance the area's economic potential many times over. And Congressman Bronson Cooper, back home to announce for re-election, had encouraging news. He had secured an order from the U. S. Corps of Engineers directing Captain William B. Wooten, the district engineer at Dallas, to inspect the Neches channel with a view toward deepening it to twenty-five feet.

The *Enterprise,* having hailed the inspecting team with warm enthusiasm, later reported hopefully that the visitors seemed to be favorably impressed. And that, in the manner of government projects since time immemorial, was that. The weeks and months passed without further word from Washington.

Will Hobby had another arrow in his quiver. If the federal government would not move, perhaps the state would. Hobby remembered an amendment to the Texas constitution, ratified five years before, which might be applied to Beaumont's problem. The legislature could now authorize political subdivisions to issue bonds for the improvement of rivers and streams, for "flood control, drainage and navigation." The authority had been used for the first two, but the navigation angle seemed to have been overlooked.

The first issue of the *Enterprise* in 1909 sketched the proposition. In a page-one editorial Hobby reiterated the tremendous benefits Beaumont would receive as a true seaport. He estimated that a deep channel would cost only $350,000, and that it would attract millions of dollars in commerce.

And Beaumont did not have to wait for the federal government to act. Under the constitutional amendment, the legislature could set up a navigation district to issue bonds for the necessary funds. Beaumont could do this job with its own money.

The proposal created a stir along the banks of the Neches. It was a new approach to an old problem, and there was no precedent by which it could be evaluated. But the more Beaumont people considered it, the better it sounded. Within a week the Chamber of Commerce voted full approval of the plan. Hobby was appointed to a committee to carry it out.

There was no time to lose. The legislature convened January 12. By dint of feverish activity, the navigation district bill was ready for introduction on the third day of the session. Hobby wanted that bill on top of the pile, hoping it could be passed before the lawmakers became involved in other pressing matters.

Beaumont quickly picked up potent support. Houston was watching the project with interest. Perhaps this was the answer to Houston's problem, too—the improvement of sluggish, meandering Buffalo Bayou, to give Houston a navigable forty-mile connection with deep water. A delegation joined Beaumont's representatives at Austin to work for passage of the navigation district bill.

To these impatient citizen lobbyists, buttonholing legislators in hotels and capitol corridors, the statehouse mill seemed to grind exceedingly slowly. Actually their bill passed in fairly expeditious fashion; on February 4, Senator E. I. Kellie of Jasper got it through the upper house, and in a few days the house of representatives approved it.

Governor Tom Campbell signed the bill into law, under an "emergency clause," on February 20. The Governor, who had watched this legislation closely and given it his unqualified support, sent the pen with which he signed the bill to Will Hobby.

Meanwhile, on the Washington level, Bronson Cooper was seeking to clear the way for an agency other than the Corps of Engineers to work on a navigable stream. Congressman Cooper was in a somewhat anomalous position in Washington; he was a "lame duck." He had been defeated for re-election by a prominent East Texas lawyer named Martin Dies. Years later the son of Martin Dies, with the same name, was to earn national recognition in the same office. In 1909 Cooper was concerned mainly with giving the Sabine-Neches project a final boost before he left office. He joined the scramble of congressmen importuning the Rivers and Harbors Committee for approval of their favorite home-district enterprises.

Cooper's task was prodigious. Reports that Senator Burton of Ohio would strenuously oppose appropriations for new projects led him to drop a proposal that the federal government pay two-thirds of the cost and local governments one-third. Instead he merely asked permission for the people of Jefferson and Orange counties to do the job, at their own expense, under War Department specifications.

There were still shoals and snags in the Washington channel, as in Beaumont's access to the sea. It came out that the Army Engineers' report of the previous year, far from being favorable as Beaumonters had hoped, actually recommended against improving the Neches River.

The ranks of home-area supporters were not entirely closed, either. The Mayor of Port Arthur and a representative of Sabine Pass were in Washington to protest the deepening of the Sabine-Neches channel, unless the canal linking Port Arthur with the Gulf were deepened from twenty-five to thirty feet.

Cooper finally wrestled his bill through the House. Senator Joe Bailey picked it up and pushed it through the Senate. His colleague, Senator Charles A. Culberson, got in a provision for a survey to determine the advisability of deepening the entire Sabine-Neches Waterway system to thirty feet all the way to the Gulf. This satisfied the Port Arthur people.

On March 2, 1909, President Theodore Roosevelt signed the bill as one of his last official acts. Cooper came home from a twenty-year career in Congress with the knowledge that his last accomplishment for the Beaumont area was perhaps his greatest. The *Enterprise* welcomed him with warm editorial praise for his record of service.

While the congressional issue was being resolved, Will Hobby kept pushing for the necessary action on the bond issue—now the sole prospective source of funds for the waterways project. A somewhat elaborate process had to be followed: The county commissioners had to be petitioned for a bond election. The court had to set a date for the Navigation Board (composed, by law, of the Commissioners' Court, the Mayor and the City Council) to consider the matter. Then the Commissioners' Court, with the board's approval, could create the navigation district and call a bond election.

To keep officials alert to the public interest and forestall any danger of community apathy, Hobby's group decided to devise still another step. On the morning of April 15, Beaumont citizens awoke to find the city plastered with signs. The mysterious legend "D.W.C. 28" in fire-engine red greeted them from every post, fence and tree. After a speculation-mounting ten days the *Enterprise* revealed the meaning of the signs: "Deep Water Campaign April 28." On that date, the *Enterprise* announced, petitions would be circulated for signatures in support of the waterway bonds.

Enterprise editorials continued to paint Beaumont's future in rosy hues, but never failed to point out that it depended

on the success of the port project. This was the hour; Beaumonters could show their interest by signing the petition.

Early on the twenty-eighth, Will Hobby was in the lobby of
the Texas Bank and Trust Company, directing a small army
of enthusiastic volunteers. The *Enterprise* had announced
that the fire siren would sound five times at eight o'clock to
signal the start of the drive. Thereafter each blast would indi-
cate that two hundred signatures had been affixed to the
petition.

Workers fanned out through the business and residential
sections. Within the first half-hour the siren screamed the
initial victory salute. Time and again it blasted forth, and
every ear in Beaumont might have been deafened if the fire
whistle had not literally blown its top off under the unusual
strain. All told, 4,075 men signed the petition. The *Enterprise*
next morning jubilantly revealed that only fifteen men had
refused to endorse the project.

The Navigation Board, duly impressed with this show of
public interest, announced its approval of the bond issue vote.
The Commissioners' Court on May 27 created the navigation
district and set a $498,000 bond election for July 8.

After the petition demonstration there was never much
doubt about the outcome of the bond election. A special
"Deep Water Edition" of the *Enterprise*—a mammoth sixty-
eight-pager—proudly announced the vote: 1,075 for the
bonds, 13 against.

A rather wistful note crept into Hobby's election story: he
had hoped for a unanimous vote of approval. But he conceded
that everyone—even those opposed to the bonds—had the
right to speak his mind.

If Beaumont people thought that Will Hobby—and they
—would be ready for a rest now, they were soon disillusioned.
Get the bonds sold and the contracts let, the *Enterprise* ex-
horted. Hobby said two courses were open: Beaumont could
go ahead on its own, or wait to see what the federal government would do and then offer its bond money as a supplement. He did not believe in waiting.

Publishers and editors of newspapers all over Texas were watching and applauding Hobby's Beaumont crusade. Editorials at Waco, Dallas and many other cities gave approving recognition to the *Enterprise*. At home, too, he was not without honor. On August 6 he was the principal speaker at a Deep Water Jubilee banquet, with Beaumont turning out in white ties and dinner gowns to hear him. Characteristically, he gave the credit to the Chamber of Commerce.

The *Enterprise* was growing financially as well as in prestige. Circulation was climbing. The special editions, besides attracting attention and favorable comment, resulted in substantial revenue gains. Another innovation was the delivery by motorcycle of the morning *Enterprise* to Port Arthur, giving Hobby's paper the largest "local" circulation territory in the state.

Everything was going well in Beaumont until Captain Waldron came to town.

It was September 7, 1909. Captain A. E. Waldron, U. S. Engineer in charge of the local district, brought along a copy of the federal law which authorized the navigation district to improve the channel. He pointed out a phrase which, he emphasized, required the War Department's full approval of each detail of the work.

That, the Captain said, meant his approval. The federal government would have to be responsible for anything that was done to the waterway; the reputation of his office was at stake. And he very much doubted, did Captain Waldron, that his specifications for the work could be met out of locally provided funds. He suggested to a roomful of startled local citizens that it would be expedient to wait for additional funds from Congress.

Then Captain Waldron went on his way, leaving consternation behind. Without Waldron's approval the navigation district couldn't put a spade in the river. His policy had to be Beaumont's policy.

It was further disclosed that Captain Waldron's report to his superiors in Washington had strongly recommended against spending any money to provide deep water for Beaumont. There was not enough local industry, he reported, to justify any improvement of shipping facilities.

The Board of Engineers and the Chief Engineer in Washington concurred in Waldron's opinion. The Rivers and Harbors Bill passed the House without any provision for the Beaumont project.

Will Hobby, representing the Chamber of Commerce, packed his bag and, on January 18, 1910, took the train for Washington.

Senator Joseph Weldon Bailey listened sympathetically to his earnest young friend and supporter. The odds were long, but Joe Bailey was a scrapper and he was for the Beaumont project. In the face of the Army Engineers' unfavorable recommendation, he induced the Senate to include an appropriation for the channel.

A conference committee of the two houses, set up to resolve the differences in their respective Rivers and Harbors bills, haggled for weeks, with the Beaumont appropriation a major issue. Senator Bailey and Congressman Dies finally had to accept a compromise proposition: a special board would reconsider the matter and report at the next session of Congress.

It was the middle of February before Hobby could return to Beaumont. Less than a month later he was back in Washington, this time for a three-month stay. With him on the mission to Washington were James F. Weed, an engineer and business leader, and Tom Adams of nearby Orange, representing the Sabine River interests.

The Texans pressed their case with the Army Engineers and with anyone else who would listen. Hobby pounded pavements and knocked on doors. He argued that deep water would bring the industries which Captain Waldron said were lacking in the Beaumont area. He quoted freight rates to show how Beaumont was discriminated against. From Houston the rate to Beaumont was three times that to Galveston, although the distance was less than twice as great. Tired but not discouraged, he returned to Beaumont to prepare for the special inspection which had been set for September.

When a five-man inspection team headed by Lieutenant

Colonel Lansing H. Beach arrived in Beaumont, after looking over the Sabine River situation at Orange, Hobby greeted
the engineers with a sixty-page special edition. For weeks he
had been urging local citizens to get their facts ready and their
arguments prepared. Now this was the day.

The engineers were escorted down the Neches on the steamboat *Kirby*. Then by auto they went all the way to the Gulf
and returned to Beaumont in the evening. At the hearing
next day they listened to a parade of Beaumont leaders citing
chapter and verse for the deep-water project.

But it remained for Governor-elect O. B. Colquitt, as the
Enterprise put it, to "save the day." As a former member of
the Texas Railroad Commission, he was thoroughly familiar
with the freight rate situation. He substantiated the local
testimony, poked the Waldron report full of holes, and showed
what port status would mean to the area in terms of industrial
development.

On October 19 came good news: the Beach report was
entirely favorable.

Local enthusiasm was further stirred by an official estimate
that the Panama Canal would be finished by December 1,
1913. Beaumont, it appeared, would be ready for the trade the
"Big Ditch" was sure to bring.

The *Enterprise* closely followed the Beach report, as it
meandered through the Washington quagmire, and heralded
its arrival on the desk of Secretary of War Dickenson on November 30. There was not enough action for impatient Will
Hobby; on December 3 he was commissioned once more for
the banks of the Potomac.

Indeed, the report had moved so slowly that the House did
not receive it in time, and its Rivers and Harbors Bill went
through again with no mention of the Beaumont project. On
December 13 the Rivers and Harbors Review Board of the
War Department granted a hearing. Hobby was there to do
what he could. Congressman Dies and George F. Burgess, of
Gonzales, a member of the Rivers and Harbors Committee,
testified for the project. It was January 20 before the board
announced its decision.

In spite of the favorable report of the inspectors and the eloquent testimony of other informed advocates, the board was still against the Beaumont project.

The blow was softened, however slightly, by the board's comment that, although it could see no justification for the proposal in terms of river traffic or commerce, there was another angle: Congress might consider it desirable on the grounds of obtaining equitable freight rates for Beaumont.

At this stage came an interlude in Beaumont's uphill battle for deep water that might have been amusing if the local citizenry had been in a frame of mind to appreciate humor. John Warne (Bet-a-Million) Gates, the barbed-wire king, Spindletop investor, founder of the Texas Company and all-round business baron of his era, had invested heavily in Port Arthur real estate and shipping facilities. He sensed that Beaumonters might be ready for a counterproposal: that they forget about improving the Neches River and simply dig a twenty-mile canal across the lowlands to Port Arthur.

Will Hobby's *Enterprise* snorted that the Gates proposal was "impracticable, not feasible, unreasonable, and essentially impossible." Hobby, the *Enterprise* and Beaumont thought Congress ought to go ahead with the original project.

Once more the load fell on Joe Bailey's broad shoulders. When the review board's unfavorable decision was announced, the Senate's Rivers and Harbors Bill was already in committee. Bailey set about the impossible-looking task of inserting an appropriation for Beaumont. He talked with every committee member. The Senator was an eloquent man, and he finally succeeded in getting an immediate $200,000 and an allocation of $371,500, all on condition that Beaumont and Orange match these sums. Against the heated opposition of Senator Burton, a staunch pay-as-you-go man, Bailey nursed the appropriation through the Senate; then he and Congressman Dies protected it through the conference committee.

There was talk that President Taft might veto the bill, but he signed it on March 1, 1911. Two weeks later it was announced that the navigation district bonds had been sold. Beaumont was ready with its part of the money.

The victory was complete, at last, and Will Hobby felt he could safely return to the business of running his newspaper. He still wrote occasional editorials with the now familiar call for immediate action. The government did not move fast enough to suit him, but in January, 1912, came the welcome news from Dallas that a contract had been let for the Sabine-Neches project. Low bidder was the Bowers Southern Dredging Company, and the total cost, exclusive of rights-of-way, was to be $652,013.90. That left some $200,000 available to cut out some of the sharp river bends and otherwise improve the channel in addition to deepening it. Actual work started in March.

Meanwhile Beaumont was growing—and so was the *Beaumont Enterprise*. Building permits, a weak $308,000 as recently as 1908, had doubled. Postal receipts followed the same pattern. Hobby led a campaign to move the Frisco Line shops from DeQuincy, Louisiana, to Beaumont. Almost daily he met with other city leaders for lunch at the Crosby House. They sought improvement of railroad service by stimulating the construction of short lines to upstate towns. They encouraged the rice experimental station, west of the city, which assisted local growers. High on their list of potential projects was a bridge across the Neches for better connections with Orange and points east.

Already nearly two-thirds of Beaumont's dusty streets were paved, and there were fifty-eight miles of concrete sidewalks. Twenty-five thousand people now lived in the Queen City of the Neches, in the heart of the longleaf yellow pine country. But oxen still pulled logs to the sawmills.

Social life in Beaumont centered around the country club, built on the site where, according to local legend, explorer LaSalle was ambushed and buried—one of a dozen-odd places in East Texas where the redoubtable Frenchman's bones allegedly rest. The Elks Club was another popular spot. As one of the most eligible young bachelors in town, Will Hobby was frequently seen at balls, parties and the theater, where formal dress was the rule and Texas gallantry was at its height. His companion at many of these functions was Miss Willie Cooper, popular daughter of former Congressman Bronson Cooper.

In February of 1912 the thirty-four-year-old Hobby was elected president of the Chamber of Commerce. It was an exciting year to be in a position of leadership, both as a citizen and as a newspaperman. It was the year that Arizona was admitted as the forty-eighth state in the Union; the Titanic hit an iceberg and went down, with 1,300 lives lost; Teddy Roosevelt bolted the Republican Party and ran for president on a third-party ticket; the Democrats balloted forty-six times before they could settle on a precise college president named Woodrow Wilson as their nominee.

In Texas, prohibition was the question of the hour. Wet O. B. Colquitt was re-elected governor over dry William F. Ramsey. Nationally and internationally, a wave of reform and liberalism was spreading. The United States vibrated to the battle cry of the suffragettes, who were rioting in London.

Locally in Beaumont, Hobby found many measures worthy of his strong editorial support. He advocated the completion of the Intracoastal Canal, which would link the Texas coast with Chicago and eventually with the eastern seaboard. He fought for municipal development of land along the banks of the Neches. He editorially condemned the downtown grade crossings which bisected the business district.

When retiring President Hobby reported on the year's work at the annual Chamber of Commerce meeting, two hundred Beaumont business leaders and their wives received his remarks warmly. There was much progress to recount. The start of deep-channel dredging was merely the foremost of many successful projects. Hobby pointed to a complete drainage survey of the county, the first of its kind in Texas. For area farmers there had been a soil analysis survey, an agricultural expert made available for free consultation, experimental stations to apply scientific knowledge to local farm conditions, and free seed in vast quantities.

Industrial plants had prospered, and the Gates handle factory had been brought to the city. A "great white way" along Pearl Street brightened Beaumont in the evenings. Two park sites had been acquired, one of which would be a permanent home for the Southeast Texas Fair. The city Dock and Wharf Commission was planning municipally-owned wharves, in anticipation of heavy demands that would come with completion of the waterway.

It was not only a bright future, but a glowing present, that Will Hobby was able to sketch for his fellow citizens of Beaumont, a thriving city only twelve years after it had been merely a dull little lumber town. The deafening applause at the conclusion of his report was partly a salute to William P. Hobby himself for his significant contributions to civic progress during the last six years.

Now Hobby turned to another phase in his developmental program for Beaumont: the expansion of rail facilities to tie in with the new channel to the sea. Rail connections with Waco, trade center of the Brazos Valley, had top priority. Frequent editorials in the *Enterprise* stressed the advantages of linking Beaumont's seaport with this agricultural cornucopia.

This concern with Waco's interests led Will Hobby to join with his brother Edwin in 1913 to buy a small Waco paper, the *Morning News*. It had competition from the afternoon *Times-Herald* and the semi-weekly *Tribune,* but the brothers believed it could be built into a valuable property. Business was slower than they had anticipated, however, and in 1914 they sold the *News* to Artemus Roberts, who thought that a prohibition paper would prosper in that predominantly Baptist community. The Hobbys cleared some $10,000 on their Waco venture. Roberts ultimately sold the paper to the Marsh-Fentress chain, which also acquired the other Waco papers.

The *Enterprise* continued to boom and by 1914 had become a genuine power in the community and the whole Southeast Texas area. Will Hobby himself had attained statewide stature as the young man who had taken a struggling little daily and created a strong and financially successful voice for progress.

6

Plunge into Politics

THE YOUNG EDITOR-PUBLISHER of the *Beaumont Enterprise* picked up his room key at the Oriental Hotel desk and started toward the stairs. It was midafternoon May 31, 1914, in Dallas.

"Will! Will Hobby!"

Several voices called his name, and he turned to face a group of friends. It was a pleasant surprise; he was in Dallas for a quiet week-end visit with his brother Edwin and hadn't expected a reception committee.

His first thought was: "Now surely I'll hear the latest political gossip." It was a red-letter day on the Texas political calendar—the last day for candidates to file for state office in the Democratic primary. And Dallas was a hotbed of political activity and influence. Hobby welcomed a chance to be "in the know," for politics still fascinated him in an impersonal sort of way.

Politics was a great game—for the other fellow. As for Will Hobby, he was more than content to observe and comment from the sidelines.

Greetings over, one of Hobby's friends came quickly to the expected subject.

"Will, we were just talking about the race for lieutenant governor. It looks as if everyone is going to drop out in favor of Senator Sturgeon. Now, the Senator is a good man, but he's a prohibitionist. We hate to see a prohibitionist win that office by default."

Hobby said he had thought of that; in fact, had carried an editorial about it in the *Enterprise*. Proponents of statewide prohibition, it appeared, were about to climb into the saddle. Tom Ball of Houston, a well-known political figure and an ardent "dry," was favored for governor over the newcomer James E. Ferguson. And now the office of lieutenant governor —important because the holder presided over the senate and would become the chief executive if anything happened to the governor—was about to fall into the laps of the "pro's" without even a token struggle.

Jim Ferguson would draw the support of the "antis" and the enmity of the "dry's," because he had announced he was opposed to any change in the liquor laws. That meant he would make no attempt to disturb the "local option" principle implanted by dry forces in the Constitution of 1876, under which many Texas counties—and precincts inside "wet" counties—had voted out alcoholic beverages.

But the prohibitionists were not content with letting each precinct write its own ticket wet or dry. They militantly demanded a statewide ban.

The issue was hotly and closely joined in Texas. The 1911 prohibition amendment had been defeated by only 6,000 votes.

Hobby said he agreed with Jim Ferguson. The prohibition issue had already taken up too much of the lawmakers' time. He agreed, too, that it seemed unfair to have no running mate for Ferguson. Even if Ferguson won the governorship, he would have a prohibitionist presiding over the senate.

"There are other things that need attention in this state," Hobby said earnestly to the little circle in the Oriental Hotel lobby. "The prohibition question ought to be laid aside. I think most of the people feel that way, too."

"We think you are right," one of the group said. "And," he added, with a smile, "I think that what you have just said solves our problem."

"How's that?" asked Hobby.

"I think you are the man to run for lieutenant governor against Senator Sturgeon."

Will Hobby was stunned. For a moment he could say nothing; then he tried to turn the proposal aside with a laugh. But he quickly saw that his friends were dead serious.

He protested that he was no orator, had no experience as a candidate and was utterly devoid of political ambition.

"Why," he said, "I can't tie a string cravat. I don't even own a swallow-tailed coat. And my hair just won't seem to grow down the back of my neck!"

Hobby's friends countered with more pertinent arguments. He knew state politics and state politicians. He was favorably known among party leaders. He had been secretary of the Democratic Party's central committee and was personally acquainted with most of the county and district committeemen all over the state. Moreover, his newspaper colleagues would support him, and the antiprohibition vote would be his.

Will Hobby did not give in easily, but after an hour he finally agreed he would follow the advice of his brother Edwin. Edwin Hobby was called to the hotel. He was even more enthusiastic than the others.

With less than an hour to spare, one of the group was sent scurrying to catch the last interurban to Hillsboro. There the name of Will Hobby was filed with party officials as a candidate for the Democratic nomination for lieutenant governor, a short while before the midnight deadline.

Hobby supporters in Dallas, going into action quickly, gave the story to the *Dallas News;* the Associated Press picked it up and distributed it statewide. Will himself called Mike Welker, his managing editor at the *Enterprise.* There was no time to announce a platform or program. That would come later, the candidate was quoted as saying.

Thus citizens throughout Texas read in their papers of June 1, 1914, of the last-minute surprise entry in the state's second-most important race. But even that story, mildly sensational as it was, could not equal for drama the untold background story: how a chance trip to Dallas to see his brother, an unexpected meeting with politically minded friends in a hotel lobby, and a brief remark that he agreed with Jim Ferguson on the prohibition question, all combined to launch a political career that was to bring to Will Hobby the highest honors his native state could offer.

And if a great many Texans were surprised to learn that there was going to be a candidate for lieutenant governor named William Pettus Hobby, their astonishment could hardly have exceeded that of the candidate himself.

Those who tried to evaluate Hobby's political assets realistically recognized that he was not cut to the typical pattern of Texas politicians. He did not possess the ringing voice characteristic of the veteran senator, Joe Bailey, or of the ambitious former speaker of the Texas house, Pat Neff, or of the bright young congressman from Marlin, Tom Connally. He did not have the height and dramatic platform appearance of the oratorical giants of that day.

Even so, he was an effective speaker. In his quiet, almost retiring manner, he was forceful on the stump. His delivery was modest and unpretentious, his voice mellow and pleasing, his manner warm and sincere. And he knew people—the rural and small-town people who lived in Polk County; the people of a bustling, fast-expanding Houston, and the citizens of a smaller but growing city, Beaumont.

Will Hobby was genuinely interested in people and their problems. He had long been a close observer and analyst of social and economic conditions, and his newspaper training had given him an invaluable background for public service. He was an astute judge of public opinion. In short, here was a new type, a new voice in Texas politics. It remained to be seen if the voting public would be receptive.

Hobby himself had no illusions as to the battle that lay ahead. If he had been overconfident, Walter Crawford soon would have set him straight.

Back in Beaumont after his intriguing announcement of June 1, Hobby was met at the railway station by admiring friends. Among them was Crawford, the lawyer who had persuaded him to move to Beaumont in the first place. And Crawford was just the man Hobby wanted to see.

"Walter," he said as they walked toward the Crosby House, "I filed for lieutenant governor with a mental reservation. It was that you would be my campaign manager."

With delight and enthusiasm, Walter Crawford immediately accepted the responsibility. Within the hour he and Will Hobby were planning a campaign.

Crawford was an experienced and sagacious political leader. He was frank with Hobby: this race would be no push-over.

In fact, Crawford continued, Hobby would have to realize in the beginning that it would be an uphill fight all the way. Senator B. B. Sturgeon of Paris was a distinguished former member of the Texas senate, the body over which Hobby was seeking to preside. They were the only two in the race, five other candidates having dropped out. Sturgeon could count on strong support from other members of the legislature, because they knew him. That support would be a major factor in Sturgeon's favor in a race that inevitably would play second fiddle to the governor's race. The former senator could be expected, too, to make as much as possible of his legislative experience in comparison with his opponent's complete lack of it.

But the most important issue of all was likely to be prohibition. Hobby had long been associated with some of the state's most prominent antiprohibitionist leaders, including Rienzi Johnston, John Henry Kirby and Senator Joe Bailey. That fact, matched against Sturgeon's militant stand for prohibition, was enough to make him, for better or for worse, the "anti" candidate.

Prohibition had been the dominant issue in Texas politics for years, emphatically so since the narrow defeat of a prohibition amendment in 1911. According to a historian of the era, "it overshadowed all other public questions and became the criterion in judging men for public office."

The "pro's" had been strong enough in the last legislature

to submit another prohibition amendment over Governor Colquitt's opposition. This amendment would be voted on, accentuating the liquor question as an issue in the various races.

Hobby was aware of this and all the other factors which pointed up the struggle ahead of him. He and Crawford first set themselves to the task of drawing up a platform. They received aid and counsel from other Beaumont friends, including Frank Keith, F. M. Law, John N. Gilbert, George M. Carroll, Emmett Fletcher and F. C. Proctor. When they had drafted the platform, they realized how similar it was to that of another inexperienced and relatively unknown candidate —James E. Ferguson, farmer, lawyer and banker of Bell County, candidate for governor against Tom Ball, the prohibition candidate, who was one of Will Hobby's good friends.

Hobby's platform announcement on June 14 had to compete for news space with the eruption of Lassen Peak in California. The volcanic action won hands down. But Hobby had come out with a constructive program.

He favored state aid to broaden home ownership; improvements in schools and state institutions; minimum rentals for tenant farmers; flood control and land reclamation; simplified civil and criminal law codes; the outlawing of campaign contributions by corporations, and a two-primary system for nominating party candidates.

Under the existing one-primary system it was possible for a candidate in a crowded race to be nominated by considerably fewer than half of the voters. Hobby urged that the two high candidates in the first primary be required to "run it off" in a second primary. This system, he pointed out, would make the eventual nominee a genuine majority, rather than a plurality, choice.

Candidate Hobby also advocated that the state senate employ counsel to write laws in plain and unambiguous language. Time after time good laws had been declared invalid by the higher courts because of equivocal wording. This proposal was to become an important point in his program.

As expected, Hobby stated that he would take no stand on the liquor question. He was convinced that it was time to subordinate the prohibition issue in favor of more important state problems. This attitude was interpreted by the prohibitionists, of course, as proof that Hobby was an "anti."

Hobby's emphasis on benefits for the laboring man and the tenant farmer, as well as his views on prohibition, linked his program closely with that of his unofficial running mate, Jim Ferguson. Essentially theirs was a team of politically untried businessmen against experienced politicians who were, furthermore, well-established leaders on the prohibition side of the state's most controversial political proposition.

As the candidates swung into widespread action, looking to the Democratic primary on July 25, many of Hobby's friends were still wondering why he wanted to run for lieutenant governor. Some of his newspaper colleagues put their speculations in print; they concluded, editorially, that they didn't understand it, but if Will Hobby wanted the job they were for him. They said Texas was fortunate to have such a man offering himself as a candidate.

The office of lieutenant governor was certainly no place for an honest man to get rich. The pay was the same as that of a member of the legislature: five dollars a day during the regular session, two dollars a day for any period over ninety days. But the lieutenant governor occupied a place of dignity second only to that of the governor. He had an influence over legislation that often exceeded that of the chief executive himself. And it was a part-time job. If Hobby won, he would not have to give up his position with the *Beaumont Enterprise*. The lieutenant governor's presence in Austin was required only when the legislature was in session.

Hobby was well acquainted with the fact that a race for lieutenant governor rarely if ever attracted public attention commensurate with its importance. This one, he knew, would be no exception; the fireworks would be reserved for the governor's race. To be entirely realistic, there would be more people intimately interested in campaigns for justice of the peace and constable than in the race for the state's second-ranking office.

With only a month in which to carry his campaign message over the vast State of Texas, Hobby decided to leave South and East Texas to his friends. He would concentrate his personal efforts in Central and West Texas, as well as in Senator Sturgeon's home area of North Texas. It would be fruitless, he decided, to bombard the newspapers with press releases. As a newspaperman, he knew they would receive little attention in view of the hotly contested governor's race.

International events conspired further to overshadow the Hobby-Sturgeon contest. Civil war was raging in Mexico. Only two weeks after Hobby announced his platform, Archduke Ferdinand of Austria and his consort were assassinated at Sarajevo. A few days later Austria declared war on Serbia. Texans tilled their fields and pondered their political choices with an eye on foreign developments. Could the United States stay out of the gathering storm? That was a more engrossing question than the selection of a lieutenant governor.

Early in July, nevertheless, Will Hobby hit the campaign trail. Wherever he found a gathering, large or small, he told his story in simple, straightforward language. Texans saw a man who neither dressed nor acted the traditional political part. But his plain talk captured their attention with its logic and sincerity. He convinced them that his platform planks were serious proposals for better government, not mere campaign generalities.

And, as his closest friends knew, that was a valid conclusion. Not being a politician at heart, Will Hobby did not deal in political persiflage or camouflage. There was no fodder in his campaign granary. His home ownership plan, for example, was part and parcel of his philosophy. He intended to do his best to see that every point in his platform eventually became a reality.

Hobby's unexpected effectiveness on the stump and the diligent organizational work of his friends headed by Walter

Crawford produced startling results. When he announced on May 31, he was a rank outsider; as primary election day neared, he had forged into the favorite's role. Hobby himself, despite his natural cautiousness, began to predict that he would beat Senator Sturgeon by 75,000 votes.

Crawford, fortunately, realized that the picture was out of focus. The prohibitionists were well organized; their quiet efforts did not always show on the surface, but they carried a potent impact. Crawford was able to convince Hobby that he shouldn't believe everything he saw and heard. It was a valuable lesson, one that Will Hobby never forgot.

The truth was that Hobby had come from nowhere to make it a terrific, close-fought race. His uphill campaign attracted thousands of supporters who had never heard of him before. And he had important friends in both factions. Leaders in both the Ferguson and Ball camps had good things to say about the Beaumont publisher, although neither candidate claimed or even mentioned him. The *Hamilton Herald,* one of the state's most ardent prohibition newspapers, came out for Hobby. It said that Hobby was a good man and advised its readers not to be too hidebound. Pro-Hobby papers quoted this comment liberally, and it impressed many prohibition voters.

The election was on Saturday, July 25. While actually it was for the Democratic nomination, in effect it was for the office itself. Democratic nominees in Texas could confidently count on winning in the general election.

Sunday's papers, except for the *Beaumont Enterprise,* reported that Sturgeon had a modest lead in the lieutenant governor's race and could be assumed to be elected. The assumption was premature. In reality Hobby and Sturgeon each had about 34,000 of the counted votes. But Sturgeon was considered the stronger in rural areas, which would be late reporting. Admittedly the outlook for Hobby was tinged with gloom.

On Monday, however, the reports showed that Hobby had spurted ahead by 3,500 votes. The margin continued to grow during the next several days until, when the unofficial vote-counting stopped, Hobby had 170,998 votes to 158,790 for Sturgeon.

Jim Ferguson had won a more resounding victory over Tom Ball, to the surprise of those political pundits who had predicted a "prohibition year." Moreover, the prohibition amendment had been beaten by a relatively wide margin.

The Democratic state convention, meeting on August 3, confirmed Hobby's nomination by adopting a resolution offered by Walter Crawford. The Lieutenant Governor-nominee responded with a brief speech in his typically modest manner. He said that only he and his brother Edwin and a few personal friends had contributed money toward his successful campaign.

"Not one cent was contributed by anyone who will ask a single favor from the legislature or from me in my official capacity," he said. "I see the dawn of a new day for Texas. If I properly interpret the election of last Saturday, it means that the people of Texas want an era of constructive statesmanship. They have instructed the next legislature and the next administration to lay aside agitation, that squabbling and quibbling, which has almost torn in twain the affairs of Texas for the last six or eight years."

Hobby referred, of course, to the prohibition unrest. To eliminate any doubt, he added, "One step of progress will follow the path of another, as surely as night follows day, and that is why I have promised the people of Texas that I will devote my time and my efforts to the material and general upbuilding of the state, and to the suspension of liquor agitation, and all those things that bring about factional and political strife."

He spoke of the need for laws that would help bring progress and prosperity to the citizens and industries of the state. This was an old story to the politically seasoned Democrats gathered in state convention, but with a new twist and flavor. They were hearing the heartfelt views of a newspaperman and businessman, rather than the elaborate rhetoric of a political orator. Here was a man who, they were convinced, was coming into office with a genuine desire to serve his state. And he had won the opportunity virtually on his own. He owed no obligation to anyone except the voters.

Within two days the eyes of Texans turned again from domestic to international vistas. The little blaze that had been lighted by Ferdinand's assassination and Austria's declaration of war against Serbia had burst into a full-scale conflagration.

Swiftly the flames spread. France declared war on Germany. Great Britain came in on the side of France. On August 4 President Wilson issued his famous Neutrality Proclamation. Every effort would be made to keep the United States out of Europe's bloody back-yard argument, but excitement continued to mount.

On the home front there was restlessness, too. In various states prohibition and women's suffrage amendments were being fought over, passed or defeated. Antitrust suits were prevalent on both national and state levels. The Panama Canal was officially opened to steamer traffic. America was stirring under a variety of tensions; there was a widespread sense of change and conflict.

It was August 17 before the statewide vote was officially canvassed. Will Hobby's margin was found to be even narrower than the early reports indicated. He had 211,197 votes to 203,441 for Senator Sturgeon. The official returns showed Hobby with a wide margin in his home county of Jefferson; in his brother's county of Dallas; in his old home county of Harris, which included Houston; and in Bexar County, which included San Antonio, then the largest city in Texas. These results were not unexpected; the real achievement had been to avert a landslide loss in the rural areas. In spite of the prohibition fever which prevailed in most of the smaller counties, Sturgeon had not been able to pick up the votes he needed to overcome Hobby's big-city strength.

Will Hobby learned, without any particular reaction of pride, that he had received the largest vote of any candidate in the general election, some 4,000 votes more than his running mate, Governor Ferguson.

By the end of 1914, the *Enterprise's* circulation had almost tripled the less-than-five-thousand figure of 1907, when Will Hobby had taken over. Besides his brother Edwin, Hobby had another new stockholder: James L. Mapes, a former Georgia and Alabama newspaperman who had come to the *Enterprise* as circulation manager. Jim Mapes had done a good job, and now that Publisher-Editor Hobby was in politics he would have an increasingly important hand in running the paper. Of the original stockholders, Crawford, Heisig and Deutser were still on hand.

Hobby was the principal speaker in November at the dedication of the Trinity River bridge at Liberty. This span connected Houston and Beaumont by highway for the first time. Hobby said the bridge would mark an era. Transportation, he reiterated as he had on many occasions, was the key to human progress. He continued:

"But the most far-reaching of all benefits that are derived from the improved public road is the encouragement it brings to land ownership and home ownership. However important other considerations may be, the progress, the happiness and the enlightenment of the farmers rest largely upon the ownership of the soil they cultivate and the independence of their homes. These are the guarantees of prosperity and the only pure and unfailing foundations of patriotism. The improved public road is the handmaiden to home ownership and land ownership, and the two become, together, the most substantial factors of progress and civilization."

In weaving this philosophy into his commemoration of the bridge opening, Hobby tactfully neglected to mention that the road between Houston and Beaumont was hardly passable when it rained—which was quite often in that section.

In December the Texas-Oklahoma Associated Press newspaper editors accepted Will Hobby's invitation to meet at

Beaumont. Harry and Perry Wiess served as hosts at the Lake View Farm, on the river north of Beaumont, owned by their father, Captain William Wiess, a leader in Neches waterways development. The occasion tied Hobby closer to his newspaper friends and probably influenced his election later as president of the Texas Associated Press Managing Editors Association.

Later that month Will and his brother Edwin went to New York on business. They stopped over in Washington to pay their respects to members of the Texas delegation in Congress. The Lieutenant Governor-elect issued a statement there intended to encourage outside investments in Texas. He defended Texas laws once called "radical" by pointing out that the same laws had been adopted by a majority of the other states and by the federal government.

In a *New York Times* interview he expanded on that subject. He said there would be a disposition to attract outside capital to Texas after he and Governor-elect Ferguson took office next January 19.

"For some years," he told the *Times* reporter, "Texas has had the reputation in financial centers of making every effort to discourage just this thing. Its drastic antitrust law, its railroad regulation extending to the issuing of securities, and its more recent law requiring insurance companies to invest 75 percent of their Texas reserves in Texas securities have been cited as instances. The last was followed by the withdrawal of most of the big insurance companies from the state."

He said he did not favor changing any of these laws, but made it plain that northern and eastern capital would get a square deal under the new administration.

"Now as to the so-called radical legislation in Texas," Hobby said, "our antitrust law has that reputation because Texas was the pioneer in this direction. Nothing can be prevented under our law that cannot be prevented under the federal Sherman Act. Texas was also a pioneer in railroad regulation. The establishment of the Railroad Commission was considered radical, but its powers have lost that aspect since those of the Interstate Commerce Commission have been increased. The insurance companies are beginning to seek readmission to Texas. The law as to investments is reasonable, and many companies had put 75 percent of their Texas funds into Texas securities even before the law was enacted."

Back in Beaumont, the Austin-bound Hobby was the honor guest at a farewell banquet. The date selected was January 10, a significant date in Beaumont's history because it was the anniversary of the Spindletop oil strike. But by 1915 the glamour of that amazing episode was fading. The thirty friends who gathered at historic old Crosby House were there to honor a young man with a future, not an oil field with a past.

Walter Crawford was the toastmaster. The occasion, he said, was a most auspicious one, for Will Hobby was the first citizen of Jefferson County ever elected to a state office.

In a prophetic toast Judge F. C. Proctor said it was reasonable to believe that Hobby would become the next governor of Texas. Will smiled at the suggestion. Such a dream was not in his mind. He wanted to be lieutenant governor for one term—possibly two, in the Texas tradition—and then retire from the political scene as a man who had fulfilled an obligation to offer for public service. He was now thirty-six years old; after two or four years he would still be a young and vigorous editor returning to the work he knew and loved best.

That was what Will Hobby thought when he left for Austin the next morning. As it turned out, Judge Proctor knew better.

7

No Opposition

JANUARY 19, 1915, was Inauguration Day. The galleries and floor of the Texas house of representatives were packed as Hobby and Senator Quintus Watson, president pro tempore of the senate, followed Governors Ferguson and Colquitt to the platform in the formal procession.

As was customary, both Ferguson and Hobby made inaugural addresses. Hobby's speech was brief and scholarly. He called attention to the war in Europe as a demonstration of the difference between an old world ruled by the ambitions and whims of emperors, kings, czars and princes, and the new world ruled by the hopes and aspirations of a whole people. He recalled the campaign pledges of the new administration and remarked how closely his platform resembled that of the incoming governor. He urged co-operation and harmony.

"The constitution of our state," he said, "has provided for three separate and distinct departments of government, emphasizing that one shall not conflict with the other. But the constitution has not provided, and the people have never proclaimed, that these three departments of government should not co-operate. So I indulge the hope that cordial relations and a common aim and a common purpose will prevail with the legislative and executive departments of the government, and that aim and that purpose will be to advance the material welfare of Texas."

Hobby's speech brought a standing ovation. Proud Beaumont citizens at the inauguration were honored, as were the members of his family, with a resolution extending to them the privileges of the senate floor for the day. Old friends were there, including John Callahan, Perry Wiess, Mr. and Mrs. Henry Roos, Mr. and Mrs. P. A. Heisig, Mr. and Mrs. Julius Wilkerson, Leon Sonfield, Walter Crawford, Mr. and Mrs. Chester Easley, L. A. Carlton, B. Deutser, Mr. and Mrs. Emmett Fletcher, Jake Giles and Mr. and Mrs. J. J. Nathan.

The new governor and lieutenant governor were hosts that evening at a formal reception in the house and senate chambers, and the traditional grand ball brought the inaugural day to an appropriate culmination. Now the Thirty-fourth Legislature could settle down to business.

And that is exactly what it did. Few legislatures in the whole history of Texas ever worked harder or in greater accord. Prohibition and other controversial issues were laid aside. The material progress of Texas, as Will Hobby had termed it, was foremost in the minds of the lawmakers and executives.

The new lieutenant governor, novice though he was in legislative give-and-take, performed like a veteran on the rostrum of the Texas senate. He occupied the presiding officer's great swivel chair with aplomb, made his committee appointments promptly, and handled parliamentary questions with confidence and dispatch. Senate members found nothing to criticize in his fair-minded decisions, handed down with a judicial dignity that had its genesis in the boyhood hours spent in his father's courtroom.

By March 20, the closing day of the session, most of the important campaign promises of both the governor and the lieutenant governor had been enacted into law. Only five bills had been vetoed by the governor. The press generally termed it the most constructive session on record.

Legislation aiding tenant farmers, laborers and the rural school children had been passed. Local governments were given authority to levy taxes for educational purposes. Improvements were made in the road program, livestock inspection and public health provisions. Important judicial reforms and higher salaries for judges were approved.

Back in Beaumont after the session, Hobby praised the work of the legislature. He listed its accomplishments in detail; then he pointed out that Beaumont and Jefferson County had fared well. Among the important benefits had been the selection of Beaumont as the location for a new court of civil appeals.

Will could now look forward to almost two years away from his official duties, barring special sessions. A week or so was given over to an inspection of the *Enterprise.* Jim Mapes had done his work well. Everything was in good order.

In Houston another newspaper had folded: the *Houston Telegram,* set up by Baldwin Rice to compete with Marcellus E. Foster's *Chronicle.* Young, handsome, aggressive Alfred Jones had been Rice's editor. When the *Telegram* went out of business, Hobby hired Jones for the *Enterprise.* The new editor took more of the load off the publisher's shoulders.

A few weeks later the *Enterprise* carried news from New Orleans that caused considerably more local comment than the usual out-of-town story. It was a report of the marriage of Willie Chapman Cooper and William Pettus Hobby.

Willie Cooper was the beautiful and charming daughter of Bronson Cooper, former congressman, long-time friend of the Hobbys. The courtship had begun while the Coopers were still in Washington, on Will's long trips there, and had continued when Bronson Cooper moved to New York in a position with the Board of General Appraisers. The blonde, blue-eyed Miss Cooper had made frequent trips to Beaumont, too, and she and the popular young publisher of the *Enterprise* had been seen together at numerous functions. Still, few people had realized that one of the city's most eligible bachelors was so close to matrimony.

The ceremony was performed at the St. Charles Hotel, with the bride's father and other members of her family present. A few couples from Beaumont, close friends, were there, including the Walter Crawfords, B. Deutser and Colonel Louis Wortham. It was widely agreed that the stately Mrs. Willie Cooper Hobby would be a distinct asset to Will in his official duties. Her years in Washington had given her a keen interest in politics, and her natural poise and tact had been enhanced by her experience in Washington society and government.

Upon their return to Beaumont, the Hobbys moved into a house on Broadway, only a few blocks from the *Enterprise* office. They were the center of a round of parties and celebrations that lasted for weeks.

Hobby found that one thing, at least, had changed in Beaumont during his sojourn at Austin. Fewer and fewer friends were calling him Will. They addressed him as "Governor," an accepted title for the lieutenant governor in informal conversation. Although Hobby would actually have preferred to be called "Will," considering "Governor" a presumptuous appellation for one who had never held the office, he offered no resistance. It lent a certain amount of dignity and prestige, and his Beaumont friends had never before been able to give a local son such a high-sounding title.

Another honor came to Hobby in November, one which his newspaper background led him to value almost as highly as his public office. The Texas Associated Press Managing Editors Association, meeting again at Captain William Wiess's Lake View Farm, elected him president.

One of his first moves was to urge the organization of what was to become known as the Texas Election Bureau. Gathering the unofficial returns of elections in such a large state as Texas was a slow, difficult and not very accurate process. Hobby had fidgeted over the tortuously slow returns in his own primary election. He recalled that the unofficial reports had given him a 12,000-vote lead, but the final official canvass cut the lead over his opponent down to less than 8,000. It would be easily possible, in a close race, for a flatly erroneous result to stand for many days until the official count was completed.

With the full co-operation of the Associated Press member

newspapers, Hobby believed, they could bring election returns to the people faster and more accurately.

The AP editors thought well of the plan. They had several months in which to perfect organization of the bureau before the 1916 primary. The step attracted little attention outside the inner circles of the newspaper business, but when election time came again the people were to realize that an important advance in public service had been made. Headquarters set up in Dallas would collect, tabulate and disperse correct election results with more dispatch than in any other state in the Union.

Early in 1916, with the war still raging in Europe, England passed the first women's suffrage bill. Hobby was interested in the movement, and his newspaper made much of its significance. A strong and growing sentiment in this country favored women's suffrage. Some of Hobby's close friends, such as Rienzi Johnston and Joe Bailey, were antisuffrage leaders, but Will himself had come to feel that women should be given the right to vote.

April 12 was a day of victory for which Beaumont citizens had long hoped and waited. On that day their city actually became a seaport.

The great Italian steamer *Lampo,* the first large ocean-going ship to traverse the Neches River channel, now twenty-five feet in depth, arrived and circled the island in the turning basin. While 6,000 people, including the school children, lined the Neches banks for a mile and cheered enthusiastically, the *Lampo* steamed into the Magnolia Petroleum Company's docks to load oil products. The four-hundred-foot ship had taken less than six hours to navigate the ship channel from the Sabine bar to Beaumont without a mishap. It was a new day for Beaumont.

As the state's second-ranking official, Hobby was in demand for speaking engagements. Early in May he went to Galveston to deliver a memorial address honoring Henry Rosenberg, the city's greatest benefactor. Rosenberg had landed in Galveston as an immigrant Swiss boy and had lived to build hospitals, schools and libraries for his adopted home. Will Hobby used the occasion to express some of his own philosophy.

"It was a fortunate combination of circumstances that linked together the life of Galveston and the life of Henry Rosenberg," he said. "It was fortunate also for mankind."

Quoting Speaker of the House Thomas B. Reed, he continued, "That divine power that creates so fixed it that one human being or one set of human beings cannot get along alone. The learned and the wise cannot be separated from the ignorant and the foolish. The brave and the strong cannot be separated from the timid and the weak. The busy and the energetic cannot be separated from the idle and the listless. The mighty and the rich cannot be separated from the humble and the poor. So it is that the brotherhood of man and the sisterhood of woman are interdependent, and if those who are lofty and able do not lift up the race, those who are lowly and helpless will drag it down.

"Natural law has decreed that we are to keep together and if we are to progress, we must do it together and nobody must be left behind. If we let the poison of filthy disease percolate through the hovels of the poor, death knocks at the palace gates. If we fail to provide education and leave to ignorance any portion of our race, the consequences of ignorance strikes us all and there is no escape. We must all move together and we must all keep together."

Jefferson County Democrats meeting in their May convention endorsed the Ferguson administration and President Woodrow Wilson. Also, somewhat to his embarrassment, they endorsed Will Hobby for governor in 1918, two years in advance. The convention resolution, moreover, echoed one adopted a week earlier by the J. G. Johnson Lodge No. 712, Brotherhood of Railroad Trainmen.

Hobby actually still had little desire to pursue politics. He was going to offer for lieutenant governor again to complete his service with the administration, but beyond that he had no political ambitions or intentions.

Jim Ferguson left the state for a few days in June and

Hobby went to Austin to act as governor. It was more of a social than an official tour of duty. Hundreds of friends from all over the state either visited him or sent messages.

The Democratic primary of 1916 arrived, with Lieutenant Governor Hobby enjoying an advantage of which office-seekers dream but infrequently attain: he had no opponent for re-election.

Governor Ferguson was less fortunate. In view of his impressive first-term record, most political observers expected him to be returned to office without serious opposition. But the prohibition issue was not dead in Texas, and the "dry's" had not forgotten or forgiven Jim Ferguson for his opposition to statewide prohibition. The Governor found himself in a bitter battle with Charles H. Morris, an East Texas banker who had been one of the minor contenders in Ferguson's first race. Morris was a lifelong prohibitionist. He charged Ferguson with extravagance and mismanagement of state funds. The race gained considerably more attention than had been expected when it started.

Ferguson was re-elected, but Morris got 172,000 votes to the Governor's 238,000, making it a relatively modest victory for a successful and popular governor seeking his traditional second term. A more serious consequence for Governor Ferguson was that doubts and questions had been created which would haunt him later.

Will Hobby and the *Enterprise* went down the line for Ferguson. Hobby also supported O. B. Colquitt in an unsuccessful race for the United States Senate against the incumbent Charles A. Culberson. He had no objection to Culberson but felt obliged to support his good friend Colquitt, who had been one of the most important and effective advocates of the Sabine-Neches Waterway.

The *Enterprise* came out with a sixty-four-page special edition in November to celebrate the opening of the South Texas Fair, which Hobby had helped to build into one of the most successful in the state. The Lieutenant Governor was the principal speaker at the opening of the fair, welcoming visitors to the city which only a month earlier had become "a magnificent fresh-water, land-locked, storm-proof harbor open to the commerce of the world."

Hobby's express views on prohibition were put on record for the first time in an *Enterprise* editorial on November 16, ten days before the prohibition of the sale of liquor in Jefferson County was to be put to a vote. Hobby said that if it were possible to stop men from drinking by passing such a local option law, that would be a different matter, but that the only result in Jefferson County would be to break local liquor dealers and enrich those of Houston and Galveston—meanwhile working a hardship on local citizens who would continue to purchase intoxicants. The prohibitionists lost the election.

Late in November, Hobby was re-elected president of the Associated Press Managing Editors Association at their meeting in Port Arthur.

The year 1917 was to prove far more fateful in the life of Will Hobby than he had ever anticipated. As the Thirty-fifth Texas Legislature prepared to convene in Austin, the war clouds of Europe were rapidly spreading westward toward the North American continent. There were ominous thunderheads gathering in Texas, too.

Jim Ferguson had not been able to shake off Morris' charges of mismanagement of public funds. In the afterglow of that fiery campaign he had weathered a preliminary investigation. But more trouble was brewing for the Governor, and the storm center was located no more than a few blocks north of his office in the capitol—on the busy forty-acre campus of the University of Texas.

8

Impeachment

JIM FERGUSON'S BRAWL with the University of Texas
began, like many controversies, on a relatively low pitch. The
original apple of discord was an appropriation bill. The state
Democratic platform in 1914 had demanded itemized appropriations for the university. Accordingly the legislature, in
1915, had passed a bill that painstakingly set out the number
of teachers in each department and the salary each should receive. The Board of Regents, however, was authorized to
make such alterations and adjustments as it might consider
necessary.

Governor Ferguson objected to this provision as an evasion
of the party edict. He signed the bill but scathingly criticized
acting President W. J. Battle and the policies of the university administration. Largely as a result of the Governor's
attack, Dr. Battle asked the Regents not to consider him for
permanent president.

The Regents further extended the olive branch by choosing
a Ferguson man as university auditor. Then they selected Dr.
R. E. Vinson as president without consulting the Governor.

When Dr. Vinson called to pay his respects, Ferguson demanded that he discharge six faculty members.

The matter rested there for a while, but by the time his
1916 campaign was over, Ferguson was committed to a fight
he could not win. He believed his responsibility as chief ex-

ecutive was involved, while his opponents regarded it as their duty to protect the university from political domination.

The Thirty-fifth Legislature opened in an atmosphere far more tense than that of the harmonious Thirty-fourth. The University of Texas issue was quickly injected. The Regents had refused to dismiss the six faculty members as Ferguson had demanded. He moved to obtain a more friendly board by making new appointments in place of three regents whose terms had expired.

At this stage, university ex-students jumped into the fray. They formed a committee headed by Will Hogg, son of the illustrious James Stephen Hogg, and demanded an investigation of the Governor's new Regent appointees. Taking up the chase, senate opponents proposed an inquiry into certain charges of misconduct on the part of the Governor. These were the old Morris accusations warmed over.

As the charges, if confirmed, would imply the impeachment of Ferguson—the bringing of an official indictment by the house of representatives, as provided in the state constitution —they were made the basis of a house resolution. An investigating committee was appointed.

Late in March, near the end of the regular session, the committee reported back, clearing Ferguson of the charges of misconduct but censuring him for certain of his actions. Ferguson's friends called the report an exoneration. The issue, however, was by no means resolved.

The turmoil in Texas over the Ferguson question, which was eventually to divide the electorate even more bitterly than prohibition, was now overshadowed by international news. During the legislative session, which had opened without ceremony because of the troubled times, the United States had moved to the brink of war. A week after it adjourned, on April 6, 1917, Congress declared war on Germany.

In the closing days of the session Will Hobby gave a clear-cut indication that he intended to retire from the state government at the end of his second term. On March 26 he accepted an appointment as director and secretary of the newly formed Federal Land Bank in Houston, which had been authorized by Congress in 1916 under the Federal Farm Loan Act.

This act was in keeping with Hobby's governmental philosophy. Its purpose was to provide long-term loans for farmers. Mortgages which bore an interest rate of 10 percent and matured in from three to five years could be replaced by the new Land Bank with 5 percent mortgage loans extending for as long as forty years. The twelve regional banks were capitalized by the federal government for $750,000 each with provision for the stock to become privately owned. This new government agency seemed intended to accomplish one of Hobby's fondest hopes, by making it possible for more and more tenant farmers to become landowners. He accepted the appointment by Secretary of the Treasury William G. McAdoo with pride and a determination to devote a major part of his time to the new assignment.

But Will Hobby's tenure with the Land Bank was to be brief. At Austin the events presaged by Governor Ferguson's troubles during the regular session were moving inexorably toward a sensational climax.

The legislature was called into special session, a few weeks after the regular session closed, to pass appropriation bills. Generous provision was made for the University of Texas, but the legislature adjourned before the Governor signed the bill.

Governor Ferguson was still demanding the dismissal of certain faculty members. The students paraded in protest, and the Regents took no conclusive action. The senate had failed to confirm Ferguson's three new appointees. A committee of the Ex-Students Association obtained an injunction restraining the Regents from discharging the embattled professors.

The Governor struck back with a heavy stroke of his blue pencil. He vetoed the university appropriation.

It was a fight to the finish now, with no-quarter flags flying from both capitol and campus. The quarrel had flared into a

statewide upheaval that vied with the World War for headlines and emotional content.

In July further fuel was heaped on the fire by a relatively
minor incident, which in more tranquil times might have attracted little attention. A board named to find a location for
another agricultural and mechanical college had met and
acted. The secretary, appointed by Ferguson, announced that
Abilene, the site strongly favored by Governor Ferguson, had
been selected.

Hobby, who was a board member, first revealed in a speech
that he had voted for San Angelo on the first ballot. F. O.
Fuller, Speaker of the House, and Fred W. Davis, Commissioner of Agriculture, then announced that they had not voted
for Abilene, either.

Hobby said he had tabulated the votes as the secretary read
them, but had not actually inspected the ballots. When the
secretary announced that Abilene had three votes in the tabu-
lation, the board then had made the vote unanimous.

The mix-up caused considerable controversy, under the
circumstances. Hobby suggested that the Location Board
simply reconvene to rectify what he called an apparent error.
There were others who took a more violent view of the incident.

On July 21, in the midst of the excitement over the University of Texas and Location Board wrangles, Governor
Ferguson appeared before the Travis County Grand Jury.
Several days later the state was rocked by the announcement
that the Governor had been indicted on seven charges of
misapplication of public funds, one charge of embezzlement
and one of diversion of a special fund.

Ferguson made bond of $13,000 and, in a typical gesture
of defiance, announced his candidacy for a third term as governor.

Now the cries for impeachment of Ferguson, hitherto confined largely to his most aggressive enemies, reached the proportions of a popular demand. The Texas constitution vests
the power of impeachment—in effect, the bringing of in-

dictments against certain high-ranking public officials—in
the house of representatives. It further provides that the impeachment shall be tried by the senate, with a two-thirds vote
necessary to convict.

On July 23, Speaker Fuller issued a call for a special session
of the house to consider impeachment proceedings against the
Governor. The constitution did not give him that specific
authority, and constitutional lawyers were divided as to the
legality of his call. After a week of indecision Governor Ferguson himself removed the doubt. He called the entire legislature into extraordinary session on August 1, for the purpose
of making appropriations for the University of Texas.

After twenty-three days of arguments and oratory, the house
adopted twenty-one articles of impeachment. Under the constitution the action automatically and immediately suspended
Ferguson from office and made Will Hobby acting governor
pending the trial in the senate.

Before taking over his duties as chief executive, Hobby re-
gretfully resigned his position with the Federal Land Bank.
On the following morning, August 24, 1917, at ten o'clock,
accompanied by his brother Edwin and his brother-in-law S.
B. Cooper, Jr., he walked into the executive offices.

Jim Ferguson received them cordially. He and Hobby
quickly effected an official transfer of executive duties.

Will Hobby did not relish his role in this tragic drama of
Texas political history. It was a delicate and trying situation
into which he had been forced. He had never desired the governorship, and certainly he did not want it under the circumstances, which denied him the prestige that goes with election to the office; his tenure was uncertain, depending entirely upon the senate's action on the impeachment charges,
and the bitterness aroused by the Ferguson fight made for
strained relationships between Ferguson's appointees and any
acting governor.

Hobby, a friend and supporter of Jim Ferguson, did his
utmost to ease the tension. He suggested that the suspended
governor continue to occupy his favorite room in the execu-

tive suite. The acting governor would content himself with less commodious quarters. Ferguson promptly accepted the offer and continued to receive friends and dictate correspondence from his regular office throughout the trial. The governor's secretary and stenographer continued to work for Ferguson, with Hobby's full consent.

Hobby installed as his own secretary Raymond Brooks, who had worked in his 1914 campaign and since had been a reporter for the *Beaumont Enterprise*. Brooks continued on the *Enterprise* payroll. Ferguson continued to occupy the Governor's Mansion; Mr. and Mrs. Hobby stayed at the Driskill Hotel.

On August 31, the last day of the state's fiscal year, Hobby signed the University of Texas appropriation bill that had played a significant role in the Ferguson case. This bill had passed in the senate while Hobby was still presiding there, but the house had not voted on it until after he had became acting governor.

On the same day the legislature started another special session, called by Hobby for five specific purposes: to attack the problem of the pink bollworm that was destroying Texas cotton, from the Mexican border eastward; to protect men called to the service from civil suits filed after enlistment; to protect the rights of soldiers in property matters; to enact legislation for drought relief; and "to facilitate a fair and impartial trial of the articles of impeachment preferred by the House of Representatives against the Governor of Texas."

Hobby's first message to the legislature was characteristically concise:

"Called temporarily to perform those duties that pertain to the Governor's Office, I have submitted or will submit for the consideration of your body the subjects that were pending at the adjournment of the Second Called Session of the Thirty-fifth Legislature; and I have convened your body at such time as will permit, with the least interruption, a final disposition of those matters. It is not necessary, therefore, for me, at this time, to encumber your duties more than is contained in the proclamation setting forth the occasion for this extraordinary session."

The session was able to accomplish all the purposes for which Hobby had called it. An additional product was an act outlining a detailed procedure for the impeachment of high state officials or judges, giving the speaker the right to call the house into session to make impeachment investigations. The legislators did not wish to be confronted again with the un-certainties that had prevailed when Speaker Fuller had issued his call a few weeks earlier.

Hobby had been importuned to offer many other matters for consideration, but he declined to do so. He took the posi-tion that an acting governor would be presumptuous to sub-mit controversial legislation or any that did not pertain to emergency matters.

Meanwhile, Ferguson's trial in the senate was making news and generating heat in historic proportions. Daily, the hos-tilities were intensified. Daily, Will Hobby met Jim Ferguson coming from the senate floor where he had been defending himself. Hobby did not participate in or even discuss the un-fortunate situation.

On September 22, the senate voted to sustain ten of the twenty-one charges against the Governor. One charge that was thrown out, ironically, was the one that had precipitated the showdown fight, a charge that he had violated the constitution in vetoing the university appropriation bill. Three other in-dictments growing out of the university controversy, however, were upheld. The senate further found Ferguson guilty of misapplication of public funds on five counts and of failure to enforce the state banking laws. The tenth charge upheld was that he had received $156,500 in currency from a source which he declined to reveal.

Three days later the senate pronounced the expected judg-ment: the Governor was removed from office and prohibited from ever holding any office in Texas. Jim Ferguson's defeat, at least temporarily, was complete.

Like prohibition, though, "Fergusonism" was not a dead

issue. Farmer Jim himself served notice of that, even before the senate handed down its formal judgment. He submitted his resignation and in the same breath reiterated his already announced intention of running for a third term as governor.

Ferguson's announcement, his burning desire to clear his name, and the implacable hatred between the Ferguson and anti-Ferguson camps combined to portend a long era of unparalleled rancor and recrimination in Texas politics.

And Will Hobby, automatically installed in the Governor's Office by the senate's action on September 25, 1917, had to face the hard fact that, by a caprice of destiny, a head-on clash with his old friend Jim Ferguson was inevitable.

9

Fill-In Governor

WILL HOBBY'S EARLY DAYS in the Governor's Office were hardly pleasant ones. The problems connected with war, drought, and pink bollworms continued to flourish, and new problems came to light each day. The legislature had spent most of its time during three special sessions with the Ferguson case, leaving important matters dangling.

Hobby was one of the youngest men ever to serve as governor of Texas. He felt the need of counsel from older and more experienced politicians. He sought, and received, advice freely during the first few weeks of his tenure.

A turning point came as the new governor stood at the window of his office in the capitol, staring out over the wide, tree-dotted lawn and thinking of the advice he had received that day. As usual, it was more confusing than helpful. One friend disagreed with another, and Hobby frankly feared that neither was right. He turned to John D. McCall, his private secretary, and Raymond Brooks, the assistant, and told them he had reached a conclusion.

"I think I am going to have to use my own judgment," he said. "I believe I can gather facts on any subject, weigh their value, use my own head about it and then do what I think is right. I can't blame anyone except myself if things go wrong, but at least I will know that I followed my own best judgment in all cases."

From that day forward Governor Hobby took his own advice. If he asked others about a matter he was considering, it was usually for information rather than recommendation.

The Governor found himself involved in a round of official duties connected with the war effort. Its climate made Texas the nation's most important military training ground. Hardly a week passed that Hobby did not have to review troops in one part of the state or another. He would be with Governor Lowden of Illinois, in Houston, or with Governor Williams of Oklahoma, in Dallas, or with a high-ranking general, in San Antonio or Austin. Liberty Loan drives brought Secretary of the Treasury McAdoo and other important officials to Texas, and Governor Hobby was expected to greet them and often accompany them on promotional tours.

It was not a time for politics as usual; however, Hobby found himself involved politically when he went to Tyler to open the East Texas Fair. Two days previously Earle B. Mayfield, a member of the Railroad Commission, had told the same crowd that he would be a candidate for governor.

Mayfield made one reservation: He would not run but, instead, would support Hobby if the Governor would call a special session and ask the legislature to pass a statewide prohibition law.

Governor Hobby opened his own Tyler speech by saying he regretted and deplored the circumstances that had resulted in his succession to the office. He added that he was willing to set an example in putting quarrels, differences and factionalism behind him in the interest of a united front against grave problems of the day.

"But," he continued, "I'd like to answer Commissioner Mayfield's offer of a political trade, made from this same platform a few days ago.

"As governor of Texas I am not open to propositions or political trades with politicians or candidates. When I get ready to trade, I will do so directly with the people of Texas and with them alone.

"Should I become a candidate for governor next year, I

will give my views on the prohibition question and my proposals on other questions. While I am serving as governor of
Texas during this national crisis, I will deal with prohibition
and all other questions in a manner that I think will be most
helpful in winning the war."

The Governor went on to say that he would administer his
office as fairly as he knew how, without prejudice, and that he
would attempt to reduce the expenses of running the state as
much as he could. As vacancies occurred in appointive positions, he would fill them with the best men available without
considering the applications of "place hunters."

Press comments were favorable on Hobby's first public address since becoming governor. One newspaper commended
him for being so far removed from "the delusions of grandeur
that characterize little men elevated to high position." Another observed that "Mr. Hobby may be with us for some
time." That was the general tenor of the comments. Few
could find fault with his speech.

The interminable and varied duties of the Governor's
Office kept Hobby's mind occupied otherwise than with
partisan politics during the rest of the year 1917. Thanksgiving Day, for example, brought a plea from the Governor for
greater sacrifices on the part of Texans in the war effort. On
that same day he appointed John C. Townes of Houston to
head the State Selective Draft Law administration.

Two days later he was looking at international problems
in another direction. Residents along the Mexican border
were alarmed over a series of bandit raids across the Rio
Grande. Hobby appointed four new Texas Ranger captains
to head four new companies recruited to cope with the situation.

Also in November, Hobby went to Washington to discuss
with President Wilson Texas' growing drought problem. December brought the submission by Congress of the 18th
Amendment, calling for nationwide prohibition when ratified
by thirty-six states. Almost immediately Texas dry forces de-

manded a special session of the legislature to close up saloons around army camps.

Shortly before Christmas the Governor announced that a committee, at his request, had toured state prisons on the lookout for deserving prisoners who had no friends or relatives to intercede for them. The result was the signing of thirty-five pardons as Christmas presents for these "forgotten men" of the Texas prison farms.

Will and Mrs. Hobby spent Christmas Day in Dallas with his mother. The first day of the new year, 1918, came and went without the usual reception at the Mansion. The Governor felt that, in view of world conditions, it was no time for social entertainment.

The year's first important official act was the Governor's meeting with the State Council of Defense and a special drought committee he had appointed, to consider relief measures. Some wanted to ask the federal government for a fifty-million-dollar grant, but Hobby pointed out that the government could not be expected to lend financial aid in view of its swollen war budget. Anyway, he said, Texas farmers would prefer to borrow money and work out their own problems rather than accept charity. It was decided to ask the federal administration to make bank deposits, as large as possible, in the 144 counties suffering from the drought.

An interesting political question was resolved on January 6, 1918, although the answer came as no particular surprise. Will Hobby announced officially that he would run for an elective term as governor.

The announcement seemed to assure at least a three-man battle for the state's highest office. Jim Ferguson, ignoring the Senate's ban against his holding office again, and Earle B. Mayfield were already announced candidates.

In his statement Governor Hobby briefly mentioned the handicaps he had worked under and said he would like to serve the people with an administration of his own. The principal plank in his platform would be to make Texas the most helpful and useful state in winning the war. Every other issue and every personal and political ambition would have to be subordinated to that effort.

Hobby shocked some of his best friends and followers by saying that he believed prohibition should be submitted to a vote, in the form of a constitutional amendment, at the regular session of the legislature in 1919. Later he elaborated on that point to correspondents by saying that he thought a majority of the people wanted to vote on prohibition, and that the federal government had urged immediate action to close the saloons around army reservations.

The Governor proposed a budget system to help cope with the increasing costs of state government; minimum wage laws for women and improved safety and sanitary conditions for all workers; and continued efforts to make it easier for Texans to own their own homes and farms. He said he would deal with all educational institutions as he had with the University of Texas after Ferguson's impeachment.

As a high point of his announcement, he revealed that the federal government had agreed to the Texas plan for placing large deposits in banks in drought-stricken counties to make it easier for hard-pressed farmers to get credit.

On all matters, Hobby concluded, in the absence of instructions from the electorate, he would continue to use his own judgment and follow his own conscience to determine what was best for Texas and Texans. Reporters who interviewed the Governor after he made his announcement came away convinced that he was determined to carry out every proposal.

The Governor then turned his attention to a department that was destined to become the largest and one of the most important of all state agencies—the Texas Highway Department. Set up in the Ferguson administration, the Highway Department had hardly begun to function. The three Ferguson-appointed commissioners found themselves unable to agree on a program. There were only a few employees and no permanent quarters. The department lacked funds, power and purpose.

Deadlocked over the appointment of a secretary to the

Commission, the incumbents accepted Chairman Curtis Hancock's suggestion that all three resign and permit Governor Hobby to name a new Commission. Hobby accepted the resignations, then reappointed Hancock and named R. M. Hubbard of New Boston and James G. Fowler of San Antonio as new commissioners. Under the revamped Commission, the Highway Department began to move, and the Hobby administration was to be remembered as the one that actually began the long struggle to "get the farmer out of the mud."

Late in January, Austin, to the astonishment of most observers, voted itself dry. To some this was calamity enough, but of greater concern to the state at large was word that the pink bollworm had spread to large areas of Southeast and East Central Texas. Hobby declared these areas under quarantine, along with the infected cotton.

Meanwhile, the political pot was beginning to bubble. Hobby Clubs started forming all over the state. One of the first was in Austin, where a famous cattleman and banker, George W. Littlefield, was made chairman of a committee to plan Hobby's Travis County campaign.

On February 2, 1918, the Governor announced he would call the Thirty-fifth Legislature into its fourth extraordinary session on February 26. He said that a committee of legislators appointed to investigate conditions and financial policies in state eleemosynary and educational institutions had reported back with important recommendations. Legislation was needed to make effective a constitutional amendment concerning reclamation districts. These districts, with proper enabling legislation, could reclaim land now unproductive and turn it to the cultivation of food and foodstuffs needed by the war machine. Several members of the legislature, he noted, had urged submission of a law to require that Democratic primary nominations be by majority vote—a proposal that had appeared in Will Hobby's original platform for lieutenant governor.

The most provocative portion of Hobby's statement was his mention of a need for laws to reach the evil of bootlegging and other vice conditions around army camps. This item brought the militant "wet's" to their feet, bristling. It had the sound of a prohibition battle cry.

When Hobby issued his formal call for the February 26 session, their fears were substantially realized. He announced that he would immediately submit laws to prohibit the sale of intoxicants for ten miles around army, navy and marine training areas. As nearly every large city in Texas had one or more of these training camps, the practical effect would be virtually to dry up the state.

Hobby's stringent proposals included making a single sale a felony and prohibiting sale to unlicensed persons or to men in uniform, or even giving liquor or procuring it for servicemen, whether in uniform or not.

His recommendations also included a special vice control law for the protection of servicemen; drought relief; the effectuation of a 1917 amendment providing for conservation of natural resources, and an adequate uniform depository law.

When the Fourth Called Session assembled, the Governor stressed the necessity of adopting laws to protect the health and morale of the armed services. He said frankly that if the state failed promptly to provide adequate safeguards, the federal government would set up federal zones around the camps and, in effect, place the major cities of Texas under martial law. He admitted that the ten-mile zone law would make almost 90 percent of Texas "dry" territory; it would be best, he thought, to pass a statewide prohibition law for the duration of the war. The courts should be directed to give liquor cases preferred consideration on their dockets. In closing his message to the legislature, Hobby read a telegram from Secretary of War Newton D. Baker urging immediate and effective measures along the lines the Governor had submitted.

It was an assignment of far-ranging scope and magnitude. The legislature's response was unparalleled.

Within thirty days it accomplished all that Hobby had asked for, in the call and in subsequent messages. Some ninety-five general laws were passed. The 18th Amendment, calling for national prohibition one year after two-thirds of the states approved it, was ratified. A statewide law was passed which prohibited the manufacture, sale or transportation of liquor anywhere in Texas. The courts later ruled that prohibition of sale was unconstitutional but upheld the manufacture and transportation ban, which was sufficient to accomplish the purpose.

Hobby had to take some scoldings for his part in the prohibition victory from old "anti" friends such as John Henry Kirby and Rienzi Johnston, the latter a state senator now. Actually, the statewide law was more a recognition of existing conditions than an instrument of great change. When it passed, 199 counties were already dry under local option; 43 others were practically dry, and only 10 counties were without dry precincts.

Kirby and Johnston were also dismayed when Hobby submitted and supported the passage of a law giving Texas women the right to vote in Democratic primaries. National women's suffrage was to come later, but the Hobby law gave Texas women practical equality with male voters in that the Democratic primary nominees were always elected in the general election. Also passed was the provision for nomination by majority vote, which meant that unless one candidate received more than half the votes in the July primary the two top candidates would have a second-primary run-off in August.

The amazing Fourth Called Session also accomplished the following: it established a commission of appeals to assist the three-man supreme court; gave counties the job of registering motor vehicles and collecting licenses; provided state aid to counties for construction of roads intended to be part of state highways; appropriated two million dollars for the purchase of feed and seed in drought-ridden counties; passed the natural resources law and most of the labor laws Hobby had included in his announcement for election; authorized the investment of state funds in short-term United States certificates to aid in the war effort; made it a felony to use disloyal language or otherwise show disloyalty to the United States during the war period; raised salaries of county school superintendents; protected the jobs of teachers who were in the armed services; provided for the redemption, within two years, of property sold for taxes; and set up standard grades of fruits and vegetables.

The session's accomplishments represented a complete victory for Texas' "fill-in" governor. Hobby's technique with the legislature had proved virtually flawless. He seldom appeared on the house or senate floors or at committee meetings. His messages, always brief and to the point, were usually presented by the speaker and the president pro tem. He observed a rule never to take the legislature by surprise, never attempt to whip lawmakers into line or usurp their functions.

Most of the laws he recommended had been discussed with members before they were submitted. Legislators frequently worked out drafts of bills with Hobby or his aides, but they remained the legislators' bills. Hobby was content with making recommendations and weaving his own thoughts into bills at the sponsors' invitation. He chose to remain in the background and let others take the credit for specific acts. It was results, not self-glorification, that he was seeking.

The mutual respect and regard between the Governor and the legislature, enhanced by these policies, bore remarkable fruit. At the end of an eventful thirty days, two facts were evident. Texas was out ahead of the other states in legislation designed to promote the war effort. And Will Hobby was the dominant figure in Texas politics.

10

"Let the People Decide"

SOME OLD-LINE Texas politicians were not convinced that Will Hobby, a modest, retiring man whose speech was straightforward and unadorned, could handle the rugged, crafty, colorful campaigner, Farmer Jim Ferguson.

The 1918 race for governor shaped up rather early as a two-man fight. Other prospective candidates, taking a second look at the two major opponents, discreetly decided to leave the field to the present governor and the ex-governor. Early in April, Attorney General Ben F. Looney withdrew his earlier announcement that he would be a candidate. The spectacular success of Hobby's Fourth Called Session was the convincer.

"Within thirty days," said Looney, "laws have been enacted which the best people of Texas have sought for thirty years. I won't run. Some people fear that if I do there will be a division among the better class of people, which division might make the way easier for evil forces."

Another whose ambition was cooled by the results of that session was Railroad Commissioner Earle B. Mayfield. He had announced his candidacy for governor months earlier. At the end of the Fourth Called Session he stated that he would not run. Later, scotching rumors that he might come back in, Mayfield said, "Under no circumstances could I be persuaded to re-enter the governor's race or consent to the use of my

84

name as a candidate as long as Governor Hobby is a candidate. The Governor has signed measures which have destroyed the liquor interests and the organized liquor machine."

That left Jim Ferguson as the only barrier between Hobby and an elective term. The senate had decreed that Ferguson could never again hold public office in Texas. Some of Hobby's friends now suggested that he take court action to keep Ferguson's name off the ballot. The Governor said he wouldn't do it.

"An issue has been drawn between Governor Ferguson and me," he would answer proponents of a ballot ban, "and the people should have an opportunity to express their preference. And they ought to have a chance to pass on my record as governor. I will accept their verdict."

Support for Hobby was rising in every section of the state. He had virtually the unanimous backing of the press. There were Hobby Clubs for both men and women in the important centers, and in some instances the sexes combined their campaigning into one Hobby-for-Governor group. This new development in Texas politics came, of course, out of the Hobby-sponsored law allowing women to vote in the Democratic primaries.

Hobby's vigorous support of the war effort was a major talking point for his advocates. It was an era when it was popular to "show one's colors" with buttons, ribbons and other decorative devices, and it was not unusual to see an enthusiastic patriot with a big button boldly proclaiming "To Hell with the Kaiser" on one lapel, and, on the other, "Hobby for Governor."

As in Hobby's original race for lieutenant governor four years earlier, his support cut across many partisan lines. Two former governors, Tom Campbell, a prohibitionist, and O. B. Colquitt, an "anti," became speakers for his cause. Both General Jacob Wolters, current head of the antiprohibition forces in the state, and Dr. A. J. Barton, Anti-Saloon League chief, were outspoken Hobby supporters. M. M. Crane, the former attorney general who had so bitterly opposed Hobby's friend

Joe Bailey in past years, became a Hobby supporter. The list included Methodist Bishop E. D. Mouzon; W. F. Doughty, superintendent of public education; E. D. Lyday, president of the State Farmer's Union; candidates running for other offices; members of the senate and house; judges of district and higher courts; and even several former state officials who had been appointed to office by Jim Ferguson.

Significantly, this type of support came spontaneously. Hobby did not seek it any more than he refused it. He remained on the job in the Governor's Office, although Ferguson already had his campaign in full swing. Hobby said he would not start campaigning until a Liberty Loan drive, beginning in early May, was successfully concluded.

Meanwhile, in April, the President called on Texas to furnish more cavalry. Governor Hobby immediately ordered the organization of two brigades, one to be commanded by General Wolters and the other by General R. H. McDill of Dallas. He also called for the organization of another infantry brigade. This was to be the new Texas National Guard, to replace guardsmen who were already in the federal service. The Governor also urged the rapid recruiting of a Home Guard composed of men outside the draft age limits.

Hobby appointed a Military Welfare Committee of distinguished citizens, with himself as ex-officio chairman, to advise with him on problems affecting the military personnel stationed in Texas. More than a quarter of a million men, a seventh of the total national force, were in Texas training camps and other stations. It was by far the greatest concentration of servicemen in the Union.

While Hobby was discharging these and other duties of the Governor's Office, his opponent was making political hay with speeches all over the state before tremendous crowds. Jim Ferguson was one of the most effective campaigners Texas ever had, and in 1918 he was at the height of his oratorical power and showmanship. He had a cause in which he thoroughly believed, that of self-vindication. Ferguson believed he had been right in his controversy with the University of Texas, and that he had been unjustly removed from office. The sincere zeal with which he pursued his 1918 campaign added much to its effectiveness.

Ferguson's approach was to attack Hobby as a "weakling" and a "political accident" and describe himself as the victim of a "conspiracy." He recounted his own achievements, which actually were many, and assailed the "autocracy" of the state university. Then he dramatically summoned the faithful to follow his banner and help him cast out the political snobs who had been his undoing.

When Governor Hobby finally took to the stump in mid-May, he counterattacked skillfully and effectively but with a minimum of personal venom. Ferguson had described Hobby as "a misfit whom God had failed to endow with the physical attributes that make up a man." And Farmer Jim made it explicit that he was talking about Hobby's short stature and big ears. When Hobby opened his campaign at McKinney, he took cognizance of Ferguson's remarks.

"I will admit that the Supreme Being failed to favor me with physical attributes pleasing to Governor Ferguson," he said, "but at least He gave me the intelligence to know the difference between my own money and that which belongs to the state."

Then he spoke seriously to his audience of 5,000 people, outlining his program, past and future, and his philosophy of public service and responsibility.

"I conceive myself to be the agent and trustee of the people," he said. "I will seek to do their will, hoping to do that which is in keeping with my individual convictions, but yielding to the supreme authority of the people always. When, according to my views, the will of the people would bring about a public wrong, contrary to my idea of right and justice, then I will yield my office, because in my judgment a public servant is a trustee and when he cannot, with fairness to his conscience, perform the trust as the makers of the trust direct, then he should give it to another to perform."

After sketching his own background as a small-town boy,

first, and then as a youth in Houston who quit school to go to work for the *Post,* Hobby declared:

"I have never received any financial favor or compensation of any sort, nor have I ever been on any payroll except that of the newspapers for which I have worked, the Federal Land Bank of Houston, and the State of Texas. I mention this, not because fees or compensation from corporations do not constitute honorable employment, but because I think it appropriate for me to say that I am under no obligation whatever for past, present, or future employment except to the people of this great state."

Hobby said he was willing to stand or fall on his record since his elevation to the governorship "under the unfortunate circumstances that occurred in the history of our state last September." These seven and a half months had been a period in which the fate of the nation, and with it that of the state, had been hanging in the balance. Texas, he pointed out, was more important to the war effort than any other state. It produced a third of the nation's cotton. It was the leader in meat production and in the combined production of wheat, corn, rice and miscellaneous food crops. It was the leader in growing feed for livestock, as well as in livestock itself. It was a major source of oil for the machines of war and of domestic production. Its long coastline and international boundary made it of tremendous military importance. Its vast extent and favorable climate had caused it to be chosen for camps in which more troops were being trained than in any other state.

"I have been guided in every thought and every act of my administration, and will continue to be guided by that which will contribute most to the success of our forces on land and sea," the Governor said. Administration of the Selective Draft Law, conservation of food, a campaign for maximum food production, and assistance in the sale of Liberty Bonds and Thrift Stamps were cited as examples of co-operation with the national government.

Another example was the legislature's passage of laws seeking to banish liquor and vice from the training areas. The ten-mile zone law, Hobby commented, had "almost settled a political issue (prohibition), so far as the legislature could settle it, which has torn this state apart for the past ten years."

And if prohibition was made to apply to soldiers, Hobby continued, it was only fair to apply it to civilians, too. "I believed it was the will of a majority of the people, evidenced by their representatives in the Texas Legislature, that the sale of liquor during the war should be prohibited by statute in this state." Thus a statewide prohibition law had been passed and signed.

The legislature, in its famous Fourth Called Session, had completed a "win-the-war" program unequaled in any other state and had given effect to the people's will on matters concerning which it had previously been "throttled."

"As a fitting climax, as a becoming crown to this program of wholesome and needed laws," Hobby commented, "the legislature provided that hereafter women shall have the right of suffrage in party nominations in Texas, thus giving the same voice in government that prevails in that most sacred and best regulated of all institutions, the American home. . . And I shall always recall as one of the proudest acts of my administration the fact that it was my privilege to approve the bill which gave women the right to vote for the first time in the State of Texas."

The primary question for the voters to determine, Hobby said, was whether the Great War was the issue of most concern to Texans. They would also determine whether the people should rule or whether "a ring of machine politicians" should again direct the government of Texas. He pounced upon a remark of former Governor Ferguson in the latter's opening speech at Mount Pleasant, where Ferguson had said that there was "an autocracy in Texas as vicious as ever flourished under the crown of the Kaiser."

"Nothing ever existed in Texas or anywhere else as vicious as the autocracy of the Kaiser," Hobby declared. He called upon the people to confirm by their votes that this was true.

Turning to Ferguson's major issue—the impeachment episode—Governor Hobby said:

"The question of next importance in this campaign is: Shall the Governor of your state obey the Constitution and the laws of the state?

"I shall not speak of ex-Governor Ferguson personally in this campaign. The other side can have a monopoly of personalities . . . I shall speak of his record as governor, however, which is public property.

"Strange to say, the issue in this campaign as it stands today is between former Governor James E. Ferguson and myself. He was tried three times and each time the verdict was against him for misuse and misapplication of the public funds of Texas. He was tried in February, 1917, found guilty and reprimanded. He was tried in August, 1917, for continuing the offenses and again found guilty by the House of Representatives and suspended from office. He was tried in September, 1917, by the State Senate, found guilty and removed from office."

The University of Texas appropriation was not a genuine issue, Hobby said. The real university issue was the question of whether the Governor or the Board of Regents should run it.

Hobby bore down heavily on Ferguson's refusal to name the sources from which he borrowed $156,000 after becoming governor. The Governor pledged that he would reveal the source of every dollar coming into his hands while in office "whenever and wherever the question is asked."

The acts leading to Ferguson's impeachment were being mentioned, Hobby said, because they were the acts of the Governor of Texas and involved a public policy upon which the people had to pass in July. "The question of his impeachment is a matter that I will leave between the ex-Governor and the legislature which passed the judgment," Hobby said.

Turning to his own program for the future, Hobby said there were three vital subjects which should command the attention of the next legislature: education, good roads and an opportunity for every person who cultivated the soil to become a landowner.

Education, he said, should begin "right down at the bottom" and go all the way to the top, and there should be equal and proportionate facilities all through the system.

"I commit myself unreservedly to the policy of extending state aid to the weaker country schools," the Governor said, adding that he would recommend an appropriation of $1,-000,000 for that purpose.

Within that overall limit, he would recommend that, where any rural school district was levying the maximum tax of fifty cents on the hundred dollars of value, the state would supplement that income, if necessary, to provide a school term "of such length as the school district desires."

"I am in favor, also," he said, "of gradually developing in the state a system under which there will be a 'state unit' for education in our common schools and every child within the state will have the same educational opportunity—that being the best."

(Thirty years later the Hobby "formula" was to be echoed in the terms of the Gilmer-Aikin Program, which provided the "minimum foundation" aid he envisioned in 1918.)

Hobby strongly urged adoption of a proposed constitutional amendment allowing an additional state tax of fifteen cents for school purposes, and for free textbooks to be supplied by the state to all children in the public schools.

As for state-supported colleges and universities, he favored "liberal financial support" and added, "In making appointments of members to serve on the various boards, I shall give them the very best talent within my power to select."

He declared for the submission of a constitutional amendment to provide state aid for the landless to buy land and homes, a measure he had favored in his first campaign for lieutenant governor.

An "aggressive and progressive policy of good roads development" under the supervision of the Highway Department was proposed, with the local, state and federal governments co-operating financially.

It was plain, straight talk the McKinney audience heard at the campaign opening, and Governor Hobby received an ovation. Some observers still doubted that the voters would appreciate the dignified approach, devoid of the political showmanship, vituperation and flamboyance to which they were accustomed, but Hobby continued to get an enthusiastic reception in town after town.

In addition to the main platform planks laid out in his opening address, the Governor subsequently mentioned other proposals: elimination of unnecessary state offices; submission of a women's suffrage amendment; judicial reform; abolition of the fee system; controls to protect renters against dangerously unsanitary conditions; strict enforcement of child labor laws; improvement of working conditions for women, with equal pay for equal work by men and women; limitation of spending in political campaigns; a budget system for the state; and further implementation of the natural resources amendment.

Governor Hobby broke off his campaign tour to go to Eagle Pass, on the Mexican border, and meet with Governor Gustavo Espinosa Mireles, the governor of Coahuila. The two executives visited both on the Texas side and in the Mexican border town of Piedras Negras. The meeting did something for the cause of international friendship and presaged a future era of good feeling after a long period of misunderstanding. More than incidentally, it did something for Hobby's campaign: Spanish-speaking Texans rallied strongly to his side.

Jim Ferguson, thrown off balance by Hobby's refusal to be drawn into roughhouse debate, occasionally grew over-anxious. He continued to draw large crowds, and he continued to snipe at Hobby. He made much of the report that the Hobbys had started building a tennis court on the Mansion grounds. Farmer Jim said he would prefer a pen for milch cows to a tennis court. This, of course, was strictly for farm and ranch consumption.

Hobby answered mildly, "It's too bad that the ex-Governor didn't think of the milch cow pen while he was in office. They say that in those days he confined his milking activities to the public treasury."

Again Ferguson, counterattacking a charge that he had opposed passage of the Selective Draft Law, pointed out that Hobby had named Jacob Wolters a brigadier general, and that on one occasion he had been introduced by former State Senator Ferdinand C. Weinert—both, he noted, of German ancestry.

It was another tactical error for Ferguson. Both the Wolters and Weinert families had lived in Texas for three-quarters of a century and were highly respected for their patriotism and integrity. The great Central Texas population of German extraction, whose forefathers had fled the fatherland to avoid persecution, resented the attack.

The one most troublesome point in the campaign for Ferguson was that unexplained $156,000 loan. Ferguson could not avoid the subject, and he refused to explain it. He said he had promised not to reveal the source of the loan and, regardless of consequences, he would keep his promise. He said he would give $1,000 to the Red Cross if Will Hobby would make the charge that the mysterious $156,000 came from the Kaiser.

Such a wild rumor had been going around, but Hobby had not repeated it. He did not believe it was true. But he did mention Ferguson's proposition to a crowd of more than 4,000 people at Abilene.

"If Ferguson wants the Red Cross to have $1,000, there is no reason for the Red Cross not to have it," Hobby said solemnly. "I will, therefore, give the Red Cross the thousand dollars if Ferguson will simply say where he DID get that money."

As the first primary election date approached, it became apparent that Hobby was far in front. Ferguson was waging a courageous and determined battle, but he was obviously losing ground. Ferguson's chances, considering the impeachment and other charges against him, hinged on his ability to get Hobby into a rough-and-tumble campaign and "muddy him up," to the confusion of the issues—and the voters.

But the tall, handsome, sharp-tongued ex-Governor could not come to grips with Hobby. He could not attack either the man or his record. And his efforts to upset Hobby with personal gibes had backfired.

During the last week of the campaign Hobby swung from North Texas to the Gulf—Bonham, Paris, Denison, Fort Worth and down to Galveston, where he made his final speech and where Willie joined him. Both candidates continued to draw crowds, but there was a significant difference: Ferguson's audiences were predominantly male, while Hobby spoke to almost as many women as men.

As Ferguson grew desperate, he stepped up his denunciations of Hobby and Hobby's supporters. He delivered a tirade against John Henry Kirby which cost him some of his leading supporters. Kirby had backed Ferguson in both his previous races for governor, but Hobby was virtually a member of the Kirby family; understandably Kirby supported Hobby. He actually was too busy to take an active part in the campaign.

(As a matter of fact, Kirby, Rienzi Johnston, Rawlins Colquitt, and other staunch antiprohibitionists close to Hobby, had threatened to turn against him if he signed the statewide prohibition and women's suffrage bills. Hobby had told them that he would sign the bills, anyway, and his old friends had thrown up their hands in disgust and said they guessed they would continue to back him even if he joined the German Army.)

The Governor went home to Beaumont to vote. On election night he stayed at the *Enterprise* office, watching the returns come in from the Texas Election Bureau by telegraph. Out front a home-town crowd gathered to follow the reports as they were flashed on a silver sheet by still projector.

Early in the evening it became evident that their honored townsman was being returned to the Governor's Office by an overwhelming vote. They set up a loud cry for Will Hobby.

Hobby responded by expressing his gratitude to the voters and saying simply that he would try to do a good job.

The final returns gave Hobby 461,749 votes to 217,012 for Ferguson. Hobby's total was the highest that had ever been cast for an opposed candidate for any office in Texas. He carried 234 of Texas' 254 counties, many of them by great majorities. One town, Red Oak in Ellis County, gave him all of its votes. And therein lay a story.

During the campaign Hobby had stepped off the train at Red Oak early one morning, planning to catch the interurban to Waxahachie. A woman in the station recognized him and insisted that he stay over for an hour so she could introduce him to the citizens of the little town. The Governor went from store to store and house to house, with striking results that were not revealed until the unanimous returns came in from Red Oak.

Hobby's victory was all the more impressive as a portent of a strong administration to come, because many members of the legislature, the lieutenant governor, and most of the elective state officials who won in the primaries had run as his friends. Ferguson appointees were resigning, and Hobby was appointing his people in their places. The beginning of his elective term in 1919 would give him an opportunity to fill many more places when terms had expired.

Will Hobby had not only a term of his own in the state's highest office; he had an official family and a legislature sympathetic with his program to support the war effort in every respect and, meanwhile, to try to bolster the Texas economy where it was sagging.

11

Wartime Governor

THE SOUTHERN PACIFIC steamed into the station at Austin, bells clanging, early on the morning of July 30, 1918. Will Hobby heard a babble of voices outside his Pullman window. He peered out and saw hundreds of people gathered on the platform. As he emerged from the car, a brass band loudly struck up "Hail to the Chief." It looked as if half of the city had turned out to welcome the Governor, triumphant in his titanic contest with Jim Ferguson.

Whistling, shouting and hand-clapping nearly drowned out the band. Dr. R. E. Vinson, president of the University of Texas, mounted a baggage truck and made a stirring speech. He described the recent election as a peaceable revolution, with Will Hobby as its leader.

A reception committee of distinguished citizens escorted Governor and Mrs. Hobby up Congress Avenue in an informal parade, with the band leading the way and enlivening the occasion with frequent outbursts of "Dixie." Early risers lined the sidewalks and enthusiastically joined in the chorus.

That afternoon the *Austin Statesman* hailed a governor who, it stated editorially, had proved that he "will not represent this faction or that; and will serve, not companions in prejudice or yoke-fellows in tradition, but the people as a whole."

Jim Ferguson was in Austin, but he did not comment on

the election. That same day, however, came clarification of the "$156,000 mystery"—the highly publicized but unexplained loan which had helped to bring about his impeachment and contributed to his defeat in the recent election.

The story came out almost incidentally in a federal income tax case. L. A. Adoue of Galveston, a former brewery president, testified that Texas brewers made the loan to Governor Ferguson in 1917 to help him straighten out his personal affairs. Adoue said it was a friendly loan made to a man who, the brewers believed, had been friendly to them.

They had feared that the gesture would be "misunderstood" and give the prohibitionists extra ammunition, so they had obtained from the Governor a pledge of secrecy. It was this pledge, apparently, that Ferguson had referred to during the campaign, when friend and foe alike were urging him to clear up the loan question.

Ironically, the information came out four days after the election, too late to help Ferguson's cause—if, indeed, it would have helped at all. Some thought that a full explanation back in 1917 might have enabled Governor Ferguson to escape impeachment.

Between the first and second primaries came an interesting ruling on the new majority election law. In the race for lieutenant governor, T. W. Davidson was runner-up to W. A. Johnson, who had campaigned on what he termed "the Hobby ticket." Between primaries Davidson withdrew. The question then was whether the third man in the race could move up into the run-off. Attorney General Looney ruled that only the second man in a first primary race was entitled to run against the leader in a second primary. Thus Johnson was the winner without further ado.

Some important odds and ends of executive business kept Hobby occupied pending the next important political event, the state Democratic convention. In August the Governor insisted that the per capita apportionment for the public schools be kept at $7.50 despite Board of Education warnings that the available school fund was dangerously low. Hobby said he would assume full responsibility for the appropriation of additional funds, if necessary, at the next session of the legislature. He had already discussed the matter with many legislators and had enough support to warrant such a commitment.

Hobby followed up the federal government's famous "Work or Fight" order, promulgated in July, with an appeal to Texas citizens to meet wartime labor demands in essential industries. The response was good, and it was unnecessary to consider enforcement measures.

There was still a drought problem, and the two million dollars appropriated, at the Fourth Called Session, for drought relief had run out. Governor Hobby decided to appeal to the public for direct donations, instead of calling another special session. He pointed out that the amount needed was hardly more than it would cost to call the legislature to Austin. His plea was favorably received and the money started coming in. Hobby appointed a citizens' advisory committee to administer the fund, with Colonel W. W. Seley of Waco as director.

The September party convention at Waco was remarkably harmonious, so much so that correspondents, missing the customary newsworthy debates and bickering, referred to it as a "love feast." Hobby forces were in almost complete control. A few dissident delegations tried to question Hobby's nomination on the basis that women had voted illegally in the primary and that their votes had provided his winning margin. This contention got nowhere, for two good reasons: Hobby's delegates had the votes to defeat it overwhelmingly, and it was without basis in the first place. His majority had been 244,000.

It was true, however, that most of the women who had exercised their new right to vote had supported Hobby. At the same time the first woman ever to offer for public office in Texas, Miss Annie Webb Blanton, had been elected state superintendent of public instruction. Mrs. Minnie Fisher Cunningham was selected by the state executive committee to be temporary chairman of the convention, which would have been another "first" for Texas women, but on the last day she declined the post because it meant she would have to be the keynote speaker. M. M. Crane—the old nemesis of Joe Bailey, Waters-Pierce and Jim Ferguson—was named in her place.

In Hobby's brief address to the convention, he observed that those who had called him a "political accident" might now refer to their own situation as a "political catastrophe." He praised the antiprohibitionists who had voted for prohibition measures necessary in the wartime crisis, and he said he looked forward to working with both sides to make Texas a model state. Again he pledged all-out support of the war effort. (As a matter of fact the war was nearly over, but that was far from evident as the fighting in Europe reached new heights of fury and the casualty lists grew longer.)

With the ceremony of the convention behind him, Governor Hobby went to Dallas for a mass meeting of Texas bankers. He managed to persuade the bankers to make substantial deposits in West Texas banks to facilitate loans to drought victims. A few days later he was calling on Texas men to register in accordance with the new draft limits of eighteen and forty-six years, as compared with the old range of twenty-one to thirty-one. The final records showed that 988,068 Texans registered during World War I, and that almost 198,000 were called into service as draftees or volunteers. The end of the carnage would leave some 5,000 of them dead on the battlefields of France.

Wartime measures occupied the Texas Governor's attention almost completely in the fall of 1918. When official Washington was reported considering the fixing of cotton prices, Hobby immediately sent a telegram urging that if such a step were taken the price be set no lower than thirty-five cents a pound. Any lower price, he said, would be disastrous to the economy of the state, as cotton was its basic commodity.

Late in September, Hobby launched the last Liberty Loan drive in Texas. He designated October 16 as Draft Day,

urging all citizens to consider themselves drafted to help out
in the bond drive. Nonessential businesses and industries
were asked to close for the day.

World events were moving swiftly. The Germans were
being driven out of France. On October 1, Bulgaria surrendered. Four days later the governments of Germany, Austria and Turkey were reported to be inquiring about armistice terms.

An end to the death and destruction of the First World
War seemed in sight. But a more deadly killer had come on
the scene. One of the greatest plagues of all time had struck
the troubled world—influenza.

Almost four out of five men in Texas military camps were
stricken, and more than 9,000—almost twice the number of
Texans killed in the war—died at Texas posts. Thousands
of civilians were dying. In Austin the toll was from ten to
fourteen daily, including some of the state's distinguished
leaders.

Governor Hobby decided to go to Washington to follow
up on his cotton pricing plea. Coming in as acting governor
was an old and special friend. Rienzi Johnston, elected to
the senate in 1916, had been named president pro tempore
at the close of the last special session. Since Hobby was the
acting governor, Texas was without a lieutenant governor;
thus, the temporary president of the senate became the chief
executive during Hobby's absence from the state.

As such, Rienzi Johnston issued a statement concerning
the influenza epidemic in which he urged the discontinuation
of all assemblies, including those in theaters, churches and
schools.

In Washington Will Hobby was conferring with President
Wilson; with Bernard Baruch, chairman of the War Industries Board; Secretary of State Lansing; General Crowder,
provost marshal general, and members of the Wartime Cotton Committee. After a twelve-day round of discussion,
Hobby was satisfied that his purpose had been achieved. He
received assurances that there probably would be no fixing

of cotton prices but if there was, the thirty-five-cent minimum would be observed.

Meanwhile, Hobby had worked out details for mustering two Texas cavalry brigades into service. To the bitter disappointment of its members, the National Guard infantry brigade was left inactive for the present. The Governor, proud of the spirit of this volunteer outfit, urged that it be given border duty, at least, as soon as possible.

A Texas governor had reason to feel at home in Washington during those days. A number of Hobby's old friends occupied high places in the government. Colonel E. M. House was the President's chief advisor. T. W. Gregory of Austin was Attorney General. A. S. Burleson, also of Austin, was Postmaster General. D. F. Houston, former president of the University of Texas, was Secretary of Agriculture. Dr. George Butte of the University of Texas was in charge of foreign intelligence for the G-2 section of the army.

Back in Texas, in late October, the Court of Criminal Appeals handed down a decision which agitated anew an old but lately quiescent problem—prohibition. The Court held that the statewide prohibition law passed at the Fourth Called Session was unconstitutional in part. The sale of liquor could not be prohibited without a constitutional amendment, and the constitution could not be set aside even for a military necessity.

Public feeling ran high against Judges W. C. Morrow and W. L. Davidson, who concurred in the majority opinion. The *Austin American* said that "a higher court, that of public opinion, has already ruled in this case and the Court of Appeals cannot overrule."

Almost overlooked in the excitement was the fact that the Court, in the same decision, upheld the portion of the law banning the manufacture and transportation of liquor. As thirsty Texans could conceive of no way to obtain alcoholic beverages without either making them or bringing them in, the practical effect was to leave the state legally as dry as the proverbial bone.

Governor Hobby himself was stricken with influenza on his return from Washington. Although his case was relatively mild, it was some weeks before he fully regained his health. He persuaded General Crowder, national draft director, to suspend the October draft because of the danger of sending new personnel into the highly infected camp areas.

October 27 brought news that Germany had asked for terms; the next day Austria surrendered. Americans prepared to go to the general election polls with the end of the war almost in sight. President Wilson's plea for a Democratic Congress was ignored and Republican majorities were elected in both houses. Hobby urged Texans to turn out and support their Commander-in-Chief, hoping for a big vote as a tribute to Wilson. But there were no local contests to bring out the voters, and no presidential election. The usual light vote was cast on November 5. Hobby received 148,982 votes to 26,713 for his Republican opponent. A Socialist candidate got about a thousand.

The Governor's real victory in that election was the approval of his Free Textbook Amendment. It carried by more than two to one.

As late as November 9, Texas was going forward with the war. Hobby designated that day for Texans to gather materials for gas masks. He joined the National Guard officers and men in their protest of a decision that they could not be shipped overseas. On November 10 the Governor got up from his sickbed to attend memorial services for Austin boys who had lost their lives in the service of their country.

That same day Hobby wrote a remarkable footnote to Texas political history, although other circumstances caused it to receive little attention. He handed to the press a list of all contributions to his campaign for governor. The total was $80,500. The largest contribution was for $11,685 made by himself and his brother Edwin. Others ranged from fifty-cents to $2,000.

Not only did the report list all contributions by name and amount; it also itemized every expenditure for mailing, ad-

vertising, travel, legal expenses, and the maintenance of headquarters in Austin, Houston and Dallas. "I have no secrets
connected with my campaign or my administration," Hobby
told the press. "I have nothing to withhold from the public."

The newspapers of November 11, 1918, had little room for
political news. Extras rolled off the presses to announce that,
in the early hours of the morning, the armistice had been
signed. Texas citizens were awakened at 3 A.M. by the shooting of shotguns, the wailing of locomotive and factory
whistles, the blowing of automobile horns and, soon, the
bedlam created by delirious celebrants parading up and down
the streets ringing bells, beating drums, blowing horns and
bawling "Over There," "Tipperary," and "K-K-K-Katy."

The war was over at last; the victory was won. Texas and
the rest of America could get their men back—some of them,
at least—and start building the new world that had been
made safe for democracy.

Not all Texans were happy, however. The National
Guardsmen who had rushed into service at General Pershing's personal request were now to be disbanded. Denied an
opportunity to serve overseas during the hostilities, they had
hoped at least to replace combat troops in the occupation
army. But by order of Secretary of War Newton Baker they
were disbanded almost as quickly as they had been organized.
Governor Hobby reported that the expense of organizing the
Guard had been borne entirely by the state treasury and
asked the federal government for reimbursement. His request
later was granted.

The Governor's Thanksgiving proclamation declared that
the world had never, in its history, had more to be thankful
for. Texans had a double reason to be grateful: their boys
were coming home, and the drought, at last, was breaking.

But influenza continued to claim victims. Before the great
plague was over it would take some 21,000,000 lives, including more than 350,000 in the United States—ten times the
number of Americans killed in action in World War I.

Early in December, after addressing a British Education

Mission at Rice Institute and a teachers' convention in Dallas, Governor Hobby went home to Beaumont to recuperate from his own bout with the "flu." A week later he was back in Austin, appointing Texas delegates to an interstate conference on taxation. Late in the month he received the resignation of F. O. Fuller, the speaker who had called the house into session in 1917 to institute impeachment proceedings against Jim Ferguson. Fuller resigned to accept a regular army commission.

Before the year was out the Governor received a report from Prison Commissioner R. L. Winfrey, who had been making an investigation at his request. Hobby said that the financial condition of the prison system was better than it had ever been, and that it was time to take the system out of partnership with private individuals by restricting its farming operations to state-owned lands.

The year 1918 had been a most eventful one for Hobby. Now, as 1919 appeared on the calendar, he looked forward to the start of his own elective term as governor. Just as he had been one of the state's youngest lieutenant governors and one of the youngest governors by succession, he would now, at forty, be one of the youngest men to assume the governor's chair by election.

With nineteen months of trouble behind him, Will Hobby was prepared to face an even greater challenge: his self-imposed assignment of making Texas "a model state."

12

"If Texas Should Go Broke—"

WILL HOBBY had reason to believe the Thirty-sixth Legislature would be a friendly one, as far as he was concerned. Many of its members had served in the famous Fourth Called Session of the Thirty-fifth, which set new high standards of co-operation between legislators and executive. And most of them, old and new members alike, had run on the "Hobby ticket" in the last election.

As Hobby stood before them on the morning of January 16, 1919, he thought and spoke of the changes that had taken place since that election. Then American troops were in the thick of battle; the country was worried and fearful; casualty lists were mounting, and no real relief was in sight. In those circumstances, Hobby commented, Texans had elected to the legislature men who, they felt, could stand up to rough times.

Now that peace had come with a sweeping military victory, this carefully selected talent could be turned to constructive tasks. The legislature and the governor could face their jobs with a buoyant spirit. Their job, he said, was to build a better State of Texas.

In Hobby's formal report on the condition of the state, he related and praised Texas' contributions to the Allied victory. But there was one development of the war period which was a cause for concern rather than commendation.

Thousands of Texans had been rejected by the services for reasons of health. Many active cases of tuberculosis, trachoma and other contagious diseases had been discovered, and the State Selective Draft Board had kept the names and addresses of the infected persons. Hobby recommended early action to raise public health standards and set up a corrective program.

The Governor said he would propose constitutional amendments authorizing ten million dollars in bonds for buildings at the University of Texas, Texas A & M College and the normal schools; allowing the state to finance small land and home purchases with low-interest, long-term loans (with emphasis upon helping returning servicemen to buy homes and farms); and combining the Supreme Court and Court of Criminal Appeals into one court of final jurisdiction in the state. He would also ask for statewide prohibition and women's suffrage amendments.

On January 21, Will Hobby finally got around to taking the oath of office as governor of Texas. He had not been formally sworn in as governor following Ferguson's impeachment. Senator O. S. Lattimore, for one, had advised against it on grounds that it might involve a relinquishment of his own elective position. Perhaps an even more persuasive deterrent was Hobby's own feeling that, in filling out Ferguson's term, he was an acting governor rather than the genuine article.

Whatever the legal and ethical niceties of the situation, they were resolved on January 21, 1919, when Chief Justice Nelson Phillips led Hobby through the quaint phraseology of the Texas oath. At Hobby's request the customary social celebration marking inaugurations was delayed until the business of the session could be well launched.

"Since I became chief executive by operation of the law of the land," Governor Hobby observed in his brief inaugural address, "it is more gratifying to me than even it would be under any other circumstances to become chief executive now by operation of the people's will."

He hoped that the legislature and the governor, working

together, might ". . . build a structure of legislation for the common good that will lighten the load of every burden bearer from the Red River to the Rio Grande and stand through all ages yet to come."

For the first time since August 1917, Texas now had a complete executive team. W. A. Johnson of Memphis, Hall County, was sworn in as lieutenant governor. Like Hobby, he was a newspaper publisher.

There would have been some justification, in fact, for calling it a "newspaper administration." Governor Hobby counted the capitol correspondents among his close personal friends and sought their counsel on his public relations problems. In addition he appointed a number of newspaper people to key positions in the government.

For example, George Waverly Briggs moved from the managing editorship of the *Galveston News* to the important post of Commissioner of Insurance and Banking. Colonel William Green Sterrett, staff correspondent for the *Dallas News*, was appointed to the Game, Fish and Oyster Commission. Jim Quarles, one of Hobby's early idols on the *Houston Post*, was secretary of the State Board of Water Engineers. Upshur Vincent, Austin correspondent for the *Post*, became chief inspector for the Fire Insurance Commission. Mrs. Frances E. Sutherland, editor and publisher of the *Smithville Times*, was named secretary of the Industrial Commission. Hobby put a Fort Worth newsman and close friend, Louis J. Wortham, on the University Board of Regents. Walter Woodul, former newspaperman and future lieutenant governor, was assistant adjutant general. And Raymond Brooks, from Hobby's *Beaumont Enterprise*, continued to serve as the Governor's assistant secretary.

The presence of these and other journalists in the administration, with Hobby's own popularity and his open-door policy for correspondents, assured a favorable climate in the daily press. Austin correspondents did not overlook or even minimize administration mistakes, but they usually reported also any extenuating circumstances.

It was appropriate that a major act of the Thirty-sixth Legislature, passed at Hobby's suggestion, was a comprehensive clarification of the state libel law. Sponsored by Representative Barry Miller of Dallas, who later became lieutenant governor, the "Bill of Rights of the Texas Press" verified and protected the rights of newspapers in reporting public meetings, official actions of public agencies and proceedings in the courts without fear of libel suits unless actual malice could be shown. It also classified as privileged matter any "fair and reasonable" criticism of the public acts of public officials.

The Thirty-sixth came close to accepting Hobby's entire list of recommendations. Thirteen constitutional amendments were submitted, including Hobby-sponsored proposals for statewide prohibition and women's suffrage. The purpose of the prohibition amendment was corrective, to bring the state constitution in line with the national. As for equal voting rights for women, these had already been provided by statute in party primary elections. A single vote was registered in opposition to these two proposals.

(When the people voted on the thirteen amendments, they turned down most of them, including women's suffrage. Hobby received the verdict with equanimity; he considered his duty fulfilled when he had suggested constitutional changes he deemed desirable. Under the constitution it was the governor's prerogative to propose; it was up to the legislature and the people to dispose.)

One of Hobby's major requests, dating back to his original platform for lieutenant governor, had been for a budget system. The legislature responded by creating the State Board of Control. The bill, by Senator Ed Westbrook of Wolfe City, set up a three-man board responsible to and appointed by the governor, to act as auditor, budget-maker and purchaser (through competitive bidding) for all state departments and institutions. The new agency also was given control of state buildings and grounds and the management of eleemosynary institutions. The bill answered another Hobby request by abolishing a dozen-odd obsolescent or useless offices.

The Governor's strongest appeal had been for adequate aid to public education, which he called "the bulwark of free government."

"While it is not necessary to urge going beyond the bounds of what the wealth and resources of Texas are abundantly able to provide," he had told the joint houses, "yet even in that event I would say that if Texas should have to go broke, let it be for the sake of education."

The legislature passed a free textbook bill, implementing a constitutional amendment adopted in 1918, and made provisions for private schools to purchase books at the state price. General fund appropriations were made for rural school and administrative aid, carrying out Hobby's campaign pledge and a plank of the state Democratic Party platform. During Hobby's administration per capita apportionment went from $7.50 to $14.50 and more than $63,000,000 in state funds was distributed for educational purposes—an unprecedented sum, and a large one in that day of high dollar values.

The single legislative act of most lasting significance was the passage of a comprehensive oil and gas conservation law authored by Senator R. L. Carlock of Fort Worth. It made "wasteful" production of oil and gas illegal, and it defined waste. The rule-making and enforcement job was left with the Railroad Commission as in a 1917 act. This law was the foundation of the present Texas conservation statutes which have been widely cited as models for the orderly development of petroleum resources. Another important law of the Thirty-sixth in this field was the common carrier pipeline act which gave oil and gas pipelines the same right of eminent domain as the railroads.

Hobby's proposed law to limit campaign expenditures was passed. Authorized expenses for gubernatorial and United States Senate campaigns were set at $10,000, a somewhat unrealistic figure to begin with as the Governor had recently reported an $80,000 outlay in his own campaign. The limit for other state and congressional races was set at $2,500.

The handling of state money deposits in banks, a source of criticism in the past, was turned over to a new State Depository Board to be composed of the state treasurer, attorney general and commissioner of Insurance and Banking.

Among the many other new laws was one regulating the practice of dentistry and setting up a board of examiners. Stronger narcotics control laws were passed. The School of Mines and Metallurgy at El Paso (later renamed Texas Western University) was made a branch of the University of Texas. The pecan was designated as the Texas State Tree. Creation of pension funds for police and firemen in cities with a population of 10,000 or more was authorized.

A law passed without Hobby's support or opposition declared that no person ineligible to hold public office in Texas should ever have his name printed on a ballot. Had such a law been on the books in 1918, Jim Ferguson presumably could not have run against Hobby for governor.

By March 3 most of the "must" legislation had been passed or was well on its way to the Governor's desk. At last the capital city of Austin could put on a party for its "new" chief executive. John L. Peeler was chairman of the inaugural committee. The membership included old friends of Will Hobby such as H. A. Wroe, M. H. Reed, Commodore E. H. Perry and Major George W. Littlefield. The historic Driskill Hotel was the scene of the inaugural ball.

A reception at the Mansion, so successful that the grand march at the hotel was delayed until eleven o'clock, was briefly interrupted by a power failure. The Hobbys brought out candles to provide the last candlelight reception in the grand old Mansion's long history.

The Hobby inaugural ball was remembered as a simple but impressive occasion. The Governor had asked that it not be over-elaborate. Following the inauguration the Hobbys made the Mansion more of a social center than it had ever been before with a series of parties and official functions.

They entertained a record number of prominent and distinguished visitors to Texas. Planned or impromptu receptions honored various organizations. One of the most notable was a reception for farm boys and girls which drew favorable comment in the state press.

Before the Thirty-sixth Legislature ended its regular term, two investigations were ordered. One had to do with the activities of the Texas Rangers, particularly in the Rio Grande Valley, and the other involved charges of voting irregularities in the same general section.

It was not surprising that complaints against the Rangers arose in the border country during 1917 and 1918. The famous force had been greatly increased in numbers during that period, and most of the recruits were stationed on the border to watch for German spies trying to enter Texas across the Rio Grande and for draft evaders trying to leave by the same route. The new men were inexperienced and, in some cases, incompetent; their activities were not always in keeping with the traditions of the Ranger service.

Two other factors contributed to the unrest. Rangers were used in an effort to enforce the prohibition law, which was not universally popular in Texas. Bootleggers and moonshiners were inclined to resent the Rangers' interference in their affairs. And it had to be admitted that a certain amount of "politics" had entered the picture. The long-established custom of making Ranger appointments from the Governor's Office invited criticism, both warranted and unwarranted.

Out of the controversial situation came a house bill by J. T. Canales of Brownsville, proposing higher pay and closer control for the Ranger force in the interest of attracting more desirable men to the service. In the course of debate over the Canales bill so many allegations were made against the Ranger force that a legislative investigation was ordered. Some of the charges were substantiated, some were not. Neither ex-Governor Ferguson nor Governor Hobby escaped criticism for "using the Ranger force for political purposes." The outcome was a bill reducing the Ranger force to four regular companies and a headquarters unit, totaling seventy-five men.

The second investigation grew out of an election contest between incumbent Senator Archie Parr of Benavides, the original "Duke of Duval," and his opponent for a second term, D. W. Glasscock of Hidalgo. Investigation of Parr's close victory margin uncovered some startling irregularities and brought changes in the election laws. In the end the senate was called upon to decide the contest, and the senators seated Parr by a vote of sixteen to fourteen.

The deciding vote was cast by Senator Rienzi Johnston, who took the position that Glasscock had not made a case and that Parr had a certificate of election. Governor Hobby took no part in the controversy. He had declined to advise Senator Johnston when his old editor on the *Post* had come to discuss it with him. Had Johnston sided with Glasscock, the election would have been "no contest" and a special election would have been necessary. Echoes of that turbulent campaign and its aftermath were heard in the capitol corridors for many years.

Near the end of the session Governor Hobby reported the results of his campaign for voluntary drought relief. More than $277,000 had been contributed and all except $4,500 had been disbursed. A total of 5,151 families had received aid. Most of the recipients insisted on signing notes, and eventually virtually all of the money was repaid. The Governor was proud to report that drought-stricken Texans were glad to get assistance but did not want charity.

13

Blue Ridge and Tidelands

IN AN ADMINISTRATION remarkably free from public censure or the breath of scandal, the "Blue Ridge Incident" was one of the few situations that brought Governor Will Hobby moments of chagrin and concern.

One of the last acts of the Thirty-sixth Legislature in its ninety-day regular session, at Hobby's suggestion, was a change in the method of purchasing land for the prison system. Hobby had renewed his plea to the legislature that the state be "taken out of partnership" with individuals who, under the existing system, worked convicts on leased farmlands under contract. He also asked for statutory guidance in the purchase of land by the Prison Commission. Several tracts were under consideration, he said, including the Blue Ridge Farm in Fort Bend County.

The legislature came through with the Raiden-Poage Bill, which virtually eliminated the convict contract system. It provided further that the commission could buy land only with legislative approval and that titles would have to be approved by the attorney general.

Hobby had said he favored terminating leases and confining prison farming operations to state-owned land. Leases could be ended either by waiving the state's option to pay rent in lieu of crops, or by exercising options to buy the land. He had not approved the commission's recommendation for buying

Blue Ridge's 5,952 acres, saying he would not do so unless the legislature approved the purchase. And now the legislature had adjourned without that approval; in fact, it had specifically denied the commission authority to make any purchase except as directed by the legislature.

Under these circumstances, when the lessor of Blue Ridge Farm proposed to terminate the state's lease and purchase option, the proposal seemed in complete accord with Hobby's views. The Governor accordingly signed a new contract shortening the Blue Ridge lease and waiving the state's option to purchase. He sent the contract to the prison commissioners at Huntsville, where two of them signed the agreement and one did not.

The ink was hardly dry on the signatures when Hobby received startling news: Gulf Oil Corporation had brought in a 1,200-barrel oil well at Blue Ridge, on the land he had just agreed to release.

It further developed that brisk lease trading had been going on around the old salt dome on Blue Ridge for some time. Neither the Governor nor the prison commissioners had been aware of the oil activity when they signed the waiver.

Governor Hobby immediately sent a letter to the attorney general describing the action that had been taken and asking for a ruling on the legality of the instrument he and two of the commissioners had signed.

In one of the longest and most detailed legal opinions on record in Texas, Attorney General C. M. Cureton held that the state had not parted with its option to purchase the Blue Ridge Farm and that steps could be taken to conserve the state's interest in the land. Thereupon Hobby called the legislature into special session for the purpose of making a final decision on the matter.

He also put in his call the purpose of passing a new soldier voting law, as the one passed at the regular session had been vetoed after the attorney general held it to be unconstitutional.

Hobby's quick action on the Blue Ridge issue forestalled,

in large measure, criticism that otherwise would surely have developed. His promptness in disclosing the full facts, submitting the question to the attorney general and calling the legislature into session left would-be critics with very little ammunition.

The legislature convened on May 5. It speedily passed a bill permitting returning servicemen to vote in the constitutional amendments election May 24 by using their service discharges in lieu of poll tax receipts, or by affidavit.

Concerning Blue Ridge, Governor Hobby said he thought the state's option to purchase should be exercised if the mineral rights were sufficiently valuable to assure a profit. He called attention to the new law requiring legislative approval of such purchases, which would be in effect before negotiations could be completed. He attached the attorney general's lengthy opinion to his message, and finally he recommended that a joint committee of the two houses be named to investigate all facts concerning the Blue Ridge incident.

The legislature passed a resolution empowering the Governor and the Prison Commission to buy Blue Ridge Farm, and it set up a committee of two senators and three representatives to make the requested investigation. Then, after five days in session, it adjourned. It was common knowledge that another session would have to be called within weeks to pass appropriation bills.

Between the first and second called sessions of the Thirty-sixth, two historic events occurred. On June 4 Congress voted to submit the 19th Amendment to the states for ratification. This was the amendment providing for women's suffrage, commonly called the Susan B. Anthony Amendment in honor of that distinguished and determined suffragette. Ten days later there was the thrilling news that two British airmen had flown nonstop across the Atlantic Ocean to the United States. Truly, the world was changing and shrinking.

At the Second Called Session, starting June 23, the legislature ran head-on into a one-man economy wave. Governor Hobby's opening message proposed trimming $4,000,000 from the biennial appropriation requests of the state departments. On the other hand, he urged that no reduction be made in educational appropriations.

Hobby pointed out that the departments had requested some $33,000,000 and that the comptroller had estimated revenue for the period at $29,000,000.

"It is easy to ask for appropriations," he said. "As the guardians of the people's money, the legislature, I trust, will make it hard to get them.

"There can be no more fitting time to watch the public expenditures with an eagle eye and safeguard them with a cautious hand. The habit of extravagant expenses is easily acquired in time of war, because cost is no consideration when it comes to the country's preservation. When the change is suddenly made from war to peace, I think the state cannot set an example more helpful, or establish a policy fraught with greater good, than a change from liberality to frugality equally as swift."

In subsequent messages Hobby asked for a state civil service system, increased salaries to go with the increased duties of the Railroad Commission, a statute to require teachers to take an oath of allegiance to the state and nation, and a law to permit the leasing of submerged coastal areas, later to become better known as the tidelands.

While the country at large was reading reports of the Versailles Treaty signing and arguing over the League of Nations, the Texas Legislature was hearing the report of the Blue Ridge Investigating Committee.

The committee dealt out criticism freely, and Will Hobby came in for a share of it. In signing the land release he had not proceeded with his characteristic caution. But the report also contained substantial commendation of the Governor for his prompt action when the oversight was discovered. All parties had acted in good faith, the committee decided. The owner had started negotiations to get his land released long before oil was found on the property. The fact was that Blue Ridge had been an oil prospect for twenty years, and min-

Knott's cartoon, promoting Hobby's election for Governor, in the *Dallas News*, 1918.

A syndicated layout which appeared in 1921 after Hobby retired from public service.

A photograph taken in the Texas Senate on February 5, 1919, as Governor Hobby signed the Texas Woman Suffrage Resolution.

eral leasing in the area was common. It was only natural that
when the oil play got a little hotter, and the governor and
legislature were taking steps to reduce prison lease holdings,
the owner should seek the return of his land.

The investigating committee went beyond the Blue Ridge
matter and commended Hobby for his parole policy. The
long-established practice of paroling convicts to private
employers had been ended. A program had been set up to
seek out deserving convicts for parole on a merit basis. The
committee recommended that paroled convicts be required to
report monthly to the Prison Commission and that the prison
system be placed on a business basis with a responsible manager to handle all transactions. At Hobby's request the legislature called for appointment of a permanent committee to
work with the Governor and the Prison Commission on
these and other suggested reforms.

The legislature also directed prison authorities to purchase
Blue Ridge Farm, by enforcing its option or by whatever
other action the attorney general prescribed. Further legislation and litigation were to keep Blue Ridge in the news for
eighteen months. In the final settlement the state acquired
the land and divided the oil and gas royalties with the former
owner. That arrangement eventually became the state's policy
in similar cases.

Meanwhile Hobby appointed his old boss, Rienzi Johnston,
to the chairmanship of the Prison Commission. It was an
appointment important enough, in Johnston's view, for him
to resign his senate seat in order to accept it.

Having disposed of the Blue Ridge controversy, the Second
Called Session turned its attention to more familiar issues—
it might be said, seemingly eternal issues—women's suffrage
and prohibition.

The 19th Amendment—equal suffrage—provided the session's major fireworks. In the regular session, the Thirty-sixth
had submitted a state constitutional amendment on that subject without a dissenting vote in either house. But on May

24, the voters of Texas turned thumbs down on women's suffrage, 166,893 to 141,773.

Now the legislature had to act on the national amendment, submitted to the states by Congress for ratification.

Even the advocates of women's suffrage in the Texas Legislature were in a quandary. They were for it; Congress was for it; Illinois, Michigan, Wisconsin, Kansas, New York and Ohio had already said they were for it—but the home folks weren't for it. Opponents made as much as they could of the anomalous situation. The people of Texas had spoken, they contended, and their decision should be sufficient for the legislature.

Governor Hobby, an ardent supporter of the amendment, spoke freely in its behalf. Without his leadership it is doubtful that Texas would have ratified the "Anthony Amendment," at least not in 1919. A proposal to postpone action until the issue could be resubmitted in a special election was beaten in the senate by only one vote, 14-13. A move to postpone consideration until the convening of the Thirty-seventh Legislature failed 17-12.

Three senators proposed that all members of the legislature resign and run for re-election at a special election, with their attitudes toward the 19th Amendment as the issue. Their resolution was promptly referred to a committee and never heard of again.

While Texas debated, Pennsylvania and Massachusetts approved the amendment. Then, on June 28, Texas became the ninth state to ratify and, to Will Hobby's delight, the first Southern state to do so.

Hobby later went to Oklahoma and Tennessee to support ratification. Tennessee was the thirty-sixth state to approve the Anthony Amendment and make it a part of the United States Constitution.

The prohibition amendment had been added to the state constitution on May 24—an almost empty gesture, as the 18th Amendment had gone into the United States Constitution five months earlier. Texas' Senator Morris Sheppard had introduced the resolution that became the 18th Amendment. All the fire was gone from the old fight in Texas. The vote on May 24th had been solidly in favor of the state prohibition amendment, but much lighter than on the suffrage amendment. Now Governor Hobby submitted the subject of an enforcement act to carry out the new constitutional provision.

The result was the Dean Act, one of the stiffest prohibition laws in the land. Sponsored by Senator W. L. Dean and eight colleagues, it was a long and involved law. It not only made the sale, manufacture and transportation of intoxicants a violation but said that the possession of alcoholic liquor for any except medicinal, mechanical or sacramental purposes was a crime against the state. Any beverage containing more than 1 percent alcohol was defined as intoxicating.

The law went so far as to say that anyone taking orders for the sale of intoxicants, or even giving information as to how or where they might be obtained, would be in violation. Any person injured in any way, accidentally or otherwise, by an intoxicated person was given the right to recover damages from all parties responsible for the intoxicated person's condition. That included those who sold the liquor, manufactured it, transported it, or told the buyer where he might obtain it. Penalty for violations was set at a minimum of one year and a maximum of five years in the state penitentiary. The Dean Act was a rugged landmark in prohibition legislation.

Most of the educational laws Hobby had requested were passed. One of the most important was a bill to finance free textbooks by setting aside fifteen cents of the thirty-five-cent tax on the hundred-dollar valuation of real property. An important oil and gas law, known as the relinquishment act, gave owners of former state lands, where the state had retained mineral rights, a one-half share of the minerals, as long as the state received one-sixteenth of the royalty.

The "tidelands," destined to become an intriguing political issue thirty years later, figured in another act of the Second Called Session. Provision was made for leasing the state-owned islands, bays, inlets, marshes and reefs within tidewater limits, as well as unsurveyed school lands and "that part of the Gulf of Mexico within the jurisdiction of Texas," for the production of oil and gas. A system of competitive bidding was set up under the direction of the State Land Commissioner.

Another law, which would grow in importance with the passing years, required the owners or operators of oil and gas wells to keep books showing production and sales. These books were open to inspection by the Railroad Commission, which could also require reports from the operators.

At Hobby's behest the legislature recognized the state's water conservation problem, with several measures. One of these enlarged the powers of water improvement districts and another authorized commissioners' courts to create water districts. This session also passed the first state law providing for the appointment of the Texas Library and Historical Commission.

With some prodding by the Governor, the two houses adopted a concurrent resolution memorializing Congress to ratify the Versailles Treaty and to follow President Wilson's plan for participation in the League of Nations. On the latter score, of course, Congress overrode Wilson, Hobby and the Texas Legislature.

As recommended by the Governor, the legislature lopped $4,000,000 from departmental requests, passed the general appropriation bill and adjourned.

In the last days of the session Governor Hobby found himself involved in another controversy brought about by an oil discovery. The scene this time was the broad, dry bed of the Red River north of Burkburnett. Texas drillers had found oil on the south bank of the river, and the south bank was the boundary line between Texas and Oklahoma. A pertinent question immediately arose: Exactly where was the south bank? Was it the water's edge or the promontory considerably south of the water? The Texas Legislature, by resolution, directed the governor and the attorney general to bring suit in the United States Supreme Court to settle the issue.

As the dispute grew warmer, there were intimations of violence. The Oklahoma Governor sent state police to the border, and Hobby countered with a contingent of Texas Rangers. A federal judge ordered Hobby to appear in his court. Hobby asked the attorney general if the governor of Texas was subject to the order. He was advised that more than likely he was.

"What can they do to me if I refuse to go?"

The attorney general said he might be cited for contempt.

"Can they actually put me in jail?"

The attorney general said they probably could. But by legal maneuvering, he further advised, Hobby could probably delay his appearance for as long as two years.

"Then I won't go," Hobby decided. "This summons orders the Governor of Texas into court—not Will Hobby. In two years I will be out of office. The next governor can have the honor."

Hobby added that the prospect might be a deterrent to some candidates, but that the field was getting a little crowded, anyway.

Finally Hobby did go to Fort Worth with Attorney General Cureton to meet the representatives of Oklahoma and the federal government. They agreed that the question was purely a legal one to be settled, as the Texas legislature had suggested, in the United States Supreme Court.

Oklahoma sued Texas, and the federal government intervened. In brief, Oklahoma claimed the entire river bed, Texas claimed the south half, and the United States disputed both claims and asserted ownership of the south half as trustee for the Indians of the several tribes occupying southern Oklahoma. Frederick Delano, an uncle of a future President, Franklin Delano Roosevelt, was named receiver for the disputed area in the interim. In 1923 the decision was finally handed down. Oklahoma got the north half of the bed, the United States got the south half, and Texas kept control of the flood plain between the banks, and thus wound up with all of the oil wells.

14

"Wilson Man"

WHENEVER Texas politicos reminisce about the tall men of past campaigns, two names inevitably will be mentioned among the first—the names of Joe Bailey and Jim Ferguson. Will Hobby, if mentioned at all, likely would be reckoned as a good governor who lacked the color of his more controversial contemporaries.

Be that as it may, the record shows that Farmer Jim Ferguson ran against Hobby for governor in 1918 and was defeated by more than two to one.

Further perusal of history will reveal that when Bailey and Ferguson teamed up against Hobby in 1920, the decision went to Hobby by approximately thirty to one.

That was Will Hobby's last personal political battle. It developed in the Democratic Party's series of conventions that marked a presidential election year. Hobby did not pick the fight with his old personal and political friend Bailey; it was forced upon him by circumstance. As for Ferguson, his part in the Democratic Party fight was coincidental. He was running for President himself on what he called the American Party ticket.

Joseph Weldon Bailey, a handsome and eloquent figure on the floor and in the committee rooms of the United States Senate, had pushed Will Hobby's Sabine-Neches Waterway legislation through Congress when all hope seemed gone. He was a great favorite of Hobby's original political confidants, John Henry Kirby and Rienzi Johnston. When Bailey resigned in a huff from the United States Senate in 1913, Governor Colquitt appointed Johnston to serve the remaining month of the term.

Will Hobby had these and other good personal reasons for not desiring a collision with Joe Bailey. For that matter, no man in his right mind would have deliberately chosen Bailey, still popular and vigorous at the age of fifty-seven, as an opponent in any political action.

Both Bailey and Ferguson bore deep political scars, but each had an almost fanatical following of considerable proportions among Texas voters. "Bailey men" and "Ferguson men" would go just about anywhere their heroes led.

The fundamental issue upon which Bailey and Hobby split in 1920 was the policies of the national Democratic Party as symbolized in the broken, embattled figure of Woodrow Wilson. Hobby was a "Wilson man." Bailey hated the very name, and almost everything the President stood for.

The break started to show as early as August of 1919, when Bailey let it be known that he felt obliged to "save the Democratic Party from itself." Jim Ferguson shared his abhorrence of the present state of party affairs but considered rehabilitation impossible. Some were unkind enough to suggest that Ferguson formed a new party because he was ineligible to appear on a state election ballot for any office. Hobby once described Farmer Jim's "American Party" as one with more leaders and fewer followers than any other political party in history. He said it was made up of "defeated candidates and broken-down politicians."

Joe Bailey would stay in the Democratic Party, working from within against the individuals and forces that, in his opinion, had wrecked it. Since 1913 he had been a bitter critic of Wilson and Wilson's policies. Now he and Jim Ferguson, acting separately but upon similar premises, leveled down in earnest on the Democratic Party and its national leadership. Unavoidably they also caught Will Hobby in their gunsights.

Bailey fired his opening blast at the little village of Covington, in northern Hill County. The occasion was an old-time Texas barbecue arranged by his admirers. The crowd was friendly and enthusiastic. There was talk of a new party to fight the decadent Democratic machine. But Joe Bailey said he would stay in the party and try to wrest control from those who favored the policies of Woodrow Wilson.

War was officially declared a few days later when Bailey attended a meeting at Fort Worth to organize for the coming convention campaign. Bailey expressed his deep-rooted opposition to the League of Nations, charged that the Democratic Party was in the hands of "semi-socialists," warned against the inroads of government on individual freedoms, demanded an end to "class legislation," and called for "separation of church and state." The last barb was directed at the political activity of men high in church affairs, especially in the various Protestant denominations.

In Houston, Bailey said he was not a candidate for any office but that he hoped to save the Texas Democratic Party. As Governor Hobby was the titular head of the Texas Democratic Party, there could be little uncertainty that Senator Bailey was delivering a direct ultimatum and challenge. He urged Ferguson's followers to give up their hopeless third party aberration and join his crusade.

Will Hobby lost no time in accepting Bailey's invitation to the political duel. At Temple in late August he spoke plainly of both Bailey and Ferguson:

"Some men never lose faith in the Democratic Party and are never fearful about the trend of public sentiment until they get beat for office or get out of office. Then they begin to doubt the capacity of the people for self-government and begin to tremble for the future of this republic."

The maneuvering and jostling continued for the remainder of the year, with the Governor taking little part. It was clear that the real battleground would be the precinct conventions early in May, 1920. The winning side there would control a majority of the county conventions, and the outcome in the counties would determine the distribution of strength in the state convention. The prize for the eventual winner would be control of the Texas delegation to the national convention, where a Democratic candidate for President would be nominated.

An interlude from state business and political pressures came to Governor Hobby in early February of 1920 when he went to Houston to welcome General John J. Pershing to Texas. "Black Jack" Pershing, famous leader of the American Expeditionary Forces, was no stranger to the Southwest; he had chased the Mexican bandit Pancho Villa persistently and unsuccessfully up and down the rugged border country while the World War was coming to a boil. The major event of the Pershing welcome was a formal banquet at which Hobby presided. Earlier in the day the Texas Governor participated in a reception at the City Auditorium, accompanied the General on a visit to Rice Institute, and was the main speaker at a Rotary Club luncheon where General Pershing and other dignitaries were honor guests.

At that gathering Hobby could not refrain from broaching the political subject that was on his mind.

"There are those," he said, "who were opposed to our entering the war, and they are kicking about everything that has happened since we got into it. They talk about their liberties being curtailed because some changes have been made in the organic law of the land, and because conditions are not exactly as they used to be. And yet, while talking about the preservation of liberty and freedom, they seldom have a word in commendation of our country for winning the war."

He added that for himself there was nothing in American history that gave him greater pride than victory in the World War under the leadership of Woodrow Wilson and John J. Pershing.

Joe Bailey, speaking in his Texas home town of Gainesville on February 18, further accelerated the political pace by announcing that he would be a candidate for governor.

He was convinced at last, he said, that he could better lead the cause of party reform if he was an active candidate. Therefore he was ending his resistance to the pleas of his supporters and taking to the hustings in earnest. He would have preferred that someone else take the candidate's role in the fight for "Jeffersonian principles." He blasted away at "the poisonous politicalism prevailing throughout the country," said he believed expenditures in Texas could be reduced tremendously at a great saving in taxes, declared himself in favor of states' rights and better educational opportunities, and attacked "aggressive labor unionism" and "denominationalism in politics."

Three other candidates had already announced for governor. Two were former speakers of the house of representatives, Pat M. Neff and R. E. Thomason. The third was Attorney General Ben F. Looney.

Governor Hobby made it plain, shortly after Bailey's announcement, that he would not be a candidate for re-election. He would have served nearly two full terms when his time was up; he would not seek another term. But he would give the people of Texas an opportunity to repudiate or endorse his administration. He would be a candidate for delegate-at-large to the National Democratic Convention.

Referring to Neff, Thomason and Looney, Hobby said, "There are candidates in the field [for governor] who are well qualified in character and ability, and who stand for those principles and those achievements which have recently made the Democratic Party, in both state and nation, so useful to mankind. I would not complicate the political situation at this time by entering a race which would confuse many of those thousands who supported me so loyally two years ago and who are now divided in their allegiance between the several candidates for governor."

Turning to the candidacy of Joe Bailey, Hobby said, "One of the candidates for governor has assailed the administration of which I am the head and the party whose mandate I hold. Having redeemed every platform pledge and promise, I am anxious for the people to determine this issue. I do not claim that I have been faultless or free of mistakes in my administration of the state's affairs. However, a program of achievements and measures that have advanced the material and moral progress of Texas, heretofore unequaled, has been put into effect.

"Therefore, not as a means of seeking political preferment, because I am too grateful for the honors already received to ask that, but as a means of seeking an expression of the people, I will be a candidate for delegate-at-large."

Bailey's candidate for the leadership of the Texas delegation to the national convention was Judge William Poindexter, who, ironically in view of Bailey's pronounced "anti" sentiments, had been one of the first prominent men to campaign for prohibition in Texas. Joe Bailey was telling his followers that the party precinct conventions would be more important than the governor's race itself.

Governor Hobby said his platform would be the policies of Woodrow Wilson and support of the League of Nations. He pointed out that the Democratic Party had wrested control of the country from Wall Street, and that farmers had received the benefit of lower interest rates and assistance in owning their own farms and homes.

The Governor said of his own stewardship: "Under my administration the doors of the University, which I found closed, have been opened, and the doors of the saloons which I found open have been closed. Prohibition has been written into the Constitution, and for the first time women have been given the privilege of voting for candidates for office; and while women have been included as participants in party primaries, aliens have been excluded from the primaries."

Hobby said that since he had been in office, the general revenue fund had attained the largest cash balance in history; record appropriations had been made for rural schools; other educational programs had progressed significantly; more state money was drawing interest than ever before; state administration had been streamlined and made more efficient; a budget system had been provided; judicial reforms had been made, and virtually every promise of his campaign and the party platform had been carried out.

"I do not assume credit for the triumphs of these measures," the Governor said. "The larger share belongs to members of the legislature who sponsored them. I only believe that upon their merit the Democrats of Texas should pass judgment as part of the achievements of my administration. I would not expect or accept the honor of serving as a delegate unless it be that the Democrats of Texas sustain and approve the achievements of the national and state democracy."

With this platform Hobby took to the campaign trail and spoke in selected areas prior to the May conventions. His opening salvo at Henderson was typical of his presentation.

"I have come to you," he said, "at a time when, in spite of the detractors of our government and the defamers of our party, human liberty has achieved the greatest triumph in all the ages, surpassing the dreams and the hopes and the inspirations of those who have fought for it in the cycle of years behind us. In that mighty and titanic struggle of the war, the Democratic Party placed its all upon the country's altar, subordinating everything to the one thing essential in time of war, service with sacrifice.

"Under the leadership of the Democratic Party our country won the war. Under the fostering care of Texas, more soldiers were trained and sent to Europe than in any other state in the Union, thus causing us, not only to feel, but to know that Texas was the most serviceable of all the states in winning the war.

"In spite of such a contribution to human liberty, toward the destruction of autocracy, toward making the world safe for democracy—when in fact thrones are tottering and monarchies are tumbling—even in that hour of supreme triumph, they have raised the cry that liberty is on the toboggan slide, and in the name of liberty and in the name of free men, they are asking you to discredit the Democratic Party and to repudiate the Democratic administration of this nation and the Democratic administration of this state."

Hobby, striking at both Bailey and Ferguson, said it was strange that men "who kept silent in the dark hour of war, when the liberty of the whole world was in peril," should suddenly become excited about the loss of liberty.

"No liberty has been lost," he said, "but only the license to sell liquor."

When the precinct conventions were held and the results tabulated, Will Hobby's last political victory had become his greatest. Out of 1,409 precincts, Bailey's forces captured only 42.

In the county conventions that followed, Baileyites won a dozen counties out of 254. It was a sweeping victory for Woodrow Wilson and the League of Nations, the Democratic Party—and Will Hobby.

Neff, Thomason and Looney, Bailey's three opponents for the nomination as governor, all favored Hobby to head the Texas delegation to the National Democratic Convention in San Francisco. But Hobby preferred to be a member of the delegation.

"I would rather receive this evidence of your approval," he told the state convention, "than to tread the ways of glory and sound all the depths of worldly political honors."

15

Right-to-Work

THE BUSINESS of the Governor's Office did not wait for Will Hobby to wind up his argument with Joe Bailey over Democratic Party affairs. In fact, at the height of that engagement the Governor had to deal with two of the most disquieting problems of his entire administration.

Both hit his desk in mid-March, just as the convention controversy was gathering momentum. On March 18, 1920, came word from Washington that the federal government was proposing to quarantine Texas cotton because of the pink bollworm blight.

The very next day Hobby learned that the busy, vital port of Galveston had been shut down tight by a dock strike.

The Governor considered his most immediately pressing problem to be the cotton quarantine. Texas was the greatest cotton producing state in the nation, and cotton was the Texas money crop. A statewide quarantine, preventing the export of any and all Texas cotton, would mean sheer economic disaster.

Already the states of Arizona, Arkansas, Florida, Louisiana, Mississippi, Oklahoma and South Carolina had barred Texas cotton at their borders; now Alabama, Georgia and North Carolina proposed to do the same. Hobby canceled several speaking engagements and departed for Washington, where a hearing was set for April 6.

Hobby had to admit that the pink bollworm had spread across the state, from the Rio Grande to the Sabine and northward. But, he told the federal authorities, a plan would be worked out to banish the pest from Texas cotton fields. He pledged his word that this would be done.

Hobby's prestige was high in the Wilson administration and his arguments were persuasive. Action was delayed on the federal quarantine.

Immediately upon his return to Texas, Governor Hobby issued a call for the Third Special Session of the Thirty-sixth Legislature. It convened on May 20, five days before the state Democratic convention. Hobby's smashing victory in the delegate-at-large fight had already been predestined, however, by the precinct and county results.

The assembled legislators heard Hobby's solemn report: The United States Department of Agriculture had served official notice that both Texas and Louisiana would be quarantined unless immediate and effective action were taken. He outlined a program of legislation which he had worked out with the federal agency, and asked the legislature to act on it with the greatest possible speed.

The response was excellent. By May 29 public hearings on the proposed legislation had been completed. The committee which conducted the hearings reported that some of the claims of the federal government had been exaggerated, but that serious infestation did exist and further steps should be taken to control the bollworm. A $1,000,000 appropriation to repay farmers for crops to be destroyed was recommended. Adequate funds were requested for the State Department of Agriculture to administer the control program, as a part of which the University of Texas and Texas A & M College would conduct scientific experiments aimed at eliminating the scourge.

Within two weeks the requested legislation had been passed, although with only a modicum of the appropriation urged by the committee. The legislature provided $50,000 for back payments to farmers, due under a 1918 law, and

$50,000 to administer the new law. It was far less than the federal government had demanded, but the program as passed was held to be adequate. Threat of federal controls was averted, and soon the other cotton states began to lift their quarantines.

The legislature completed its original assignment with such dispatch that Hobby decided to submit other subjects. The treasury showed a $6,000,000 balance, and the Governor suggested that schoolteachers be given an overdue raise. This was done at a cost of $4,000,000. Another million was added to the higher education appropriation. The remaining million was distributed for emergency uses by state departments and institutions.

A resolution adopted by the legislature called for moving the University Medical School from Galveston. The reason given was that not enough clinical material was available on the Island. The resolution had no practical effect, as a constitutional amendment would have been required to relocate the school.

An important act was that which placed gas utilities under the control of the Railroad Commission. Dr. George Butte was appointed by Hobby to set up the rules and regulations. The brilliant University of Texas professor had performed a similar service when the oil and gas division was established. Educated at the University of Texas, Austin College, University of Berlin, Heidelberg and Ecole de Droit in France, Dr. Butte had served during the war as director of foreign intelligence for the War Department general staff. In later years he was to become dean of the University School of Law, a candidate for governor on the Republican ticket, attorney general of Puerto Rico, acting governor of the Philippines and associate justice of the Supreme Court of the Philippines.

Will Hobby always had a high regard for George Butte, despite the fact that he was one of the state's leading Republicans.

Strike violence at Galveston had been increasing. The legislature, at Hobby's request, appropriated $100,000 to pay expenses of the National Guard should the Governor find it necessary to proclaim martial law.

And that time was not far in the future. The Galveston situation was out of control. A strike that had started on orders from a New York union, largely in sympathy with New York port workers, had become a bitter gang-type war on the freight-clogged docks. It was reported that Galveston authorities, concerned over the political power of the unions, were slow to interfere even when physical violence was used against the strikebreakers who were being imported by the shipping companies.

The explosive situation was rendered all the more dangerous by a racial angle. Some of the strikers were Negroes; some of the strikebreakers were whites. Reports spread over the state that race riots were imminent. White vigilante groups started forming in nearby areas. Governor Hobby warned the Galveston mayor and city commissioners that, unless the city took effective action immediately, the state would have to act. The warning was apparently ignored then, but soon even the mayor was calling for help.

A mob had attacked an interurban from Houston. Clubs were swung freely, and shots rang out inside the car. Hobby sent in four Rangers, but even those indomitable officers could not handle the situation without co-operation from local police. After a survey, the adjutant general pronounced the situation hopeless without state interference. Hobby immediately proclaimed a state of martial law on Galveston Island.

The order became effective on the morning of June 7, 1920. General Jacob Wolters proceeded to Galveston with elements of four National Guard regiments, including three machine gun companies, four companies of cavalry and a medical detachment. His first order forbade the sale or carrying of firearms, interfering with workers, congregating and loitering. He ordered the arrest of all idlers and told the merchants to reopen their shops and carry on normal business.

The following day the rest of the large militia force reached the city and established a camp on the beach. Patrol zones were set up. All gambling, prostitution and other forms of vice were closed down. The prohibition law was strictly enforced, and sentries went on twenty-four-hour duty throughout the city and its environs. Within hours after the guardsmen took their stations, disorder ceased and the Island was quiet.

Under the watchful eye of the troops, longshoremen tackled the huge mountains of freight that had been collecting since the middle of March. In three weeks, 8,700 tons had been moved out of the Port of Galveston.

Bitter clashes between the workers and their sympathizers on both sides still flared now and then, but the situation grew calmer and the National Guard forces were gradually withdrawn, until by early July they numbered only fifty officers and 450 men. Unfortunately, as the troops left, the local police fell back into their old habit of ignoring the activities of union "enforcers." It became apparent that the situation was growing worse instead of better, and Hobby again stepped in.

He issued, on July 14, a supplementary proclamation suspending from office the police judge, police chief, chief of detectives and the entire city police and detective forces, for failure to enforce the law and for obstruction of the state's efforts. The mayor, commissioners and city attorney were allowed to continue their routine duties but were denied any jurisdiction in the enforcement of penal laws.

General Wolters took charge of all jails and courts and ordered the disarming of the police. He appointed Colonel A. W. Bloor provost marshal and Captain O'Brien Stevens judge advocate.

The mayor and city commissioners filed a suit against the governor and General Wolters, but it was immediately dismissed by the district judge. A second court test came when a citizen, arrested by the military for speeding, challenged the validity of martial law in federal district court. Federal Judge R. E. Foster sustained the governor's proclamation.

The "military occupation" of Galveston finally brought

peace, and continued negotiations between state and local authorities eventually resulted in an agreement which justified recalling the state troops. Hobby accepted the proposal of Galveston city officials and church, business and labor leaders that he appoint a Ranger captain to exercise complete control and authority over all peace officers on the Island with the help of as many Rangers as he believed necessary. The city fathers pledged that they would remove permanently from the force any police officer who failed to co-operate with or obey the orders of the Ranger captain. A representative committee would act as an advisory group to assist in law enforcement and to work toward a better understanding between laborers and employers.

Hobby accepted the plan as soon as the city ratified it. In his announcement ending martial law and restoring the Island government to the civil authorities, he said that he had taken no sides in the strike other than to extend protection to all persons in pursuit of their constitutional rights.

"Those employed at the port will be given the same protection as heretofore," he said, "because if this agreement is not carried out in good faith, and if there is any hindrance or interference with the Rangers through local authorities, I will immediately take the necessary steps to give protection, even if martial law and the return of soldiers is necessary."

At midnight, September 30, National Guard authorities turned over their responsibilities to Ranger Captain Joe B. Brooks.

Thus ended an exciting chapter in the colorful saga of Galveston. The martial law period had passed with a minimum of violent overtones. There had been only one fatality, the accidental shooting of a National Guard captain by a sentry. The most embarrassing incident, for Hobby, grew out of the overzealous efforts of Colonel Billie Mayfield and three subordinate officers to arrest a critical newspaper editor in Houston, fifty miles from the martial law zone. Even Hobby's friendly newspaper colleagues roundly denounced this abortive expedition.

By and large, however, the state press was highly commendatory of Governor Hobby for his handling of the Galveston affair. The *San Antonio Express* stated the consensus: ". . . The closing of the drama of the longshoremen's strike in Galveston is striking illustration of how a strong man in the Governor's Office may perform a disagreeable duty so well that the lesson may be thoroughly learned."

Even the citizens of Galveston felt substantial good will, at the finish, toward the uninvited visitors in uniform. Contributing to this feeling were the heroic efforts of guardsmen in controlling two serious warehouse fires that broke out near the close of the occupation. They saved millions of dollars' worth of goods and probably kept the entire water front from going up in flames. Any remaining ill will vanished, and the end of martial law was observed with a series of banquets given by Galveston people for the guardsmen.

Meanwhile, Governor Hobby had the Texas Legislature in session again, for the primary purpose of dealing with women's suffrage. Women had been granted the right to vote in the approaching general election; yet, in Texas, there had not been time for them to qualify for voting by payment of poll taxes. The session began on September 21 and ended October 2, with the problem solved by extending the poll tax payment deadline to October 22. The word "male" was eliminated from all statutes relating to the poll tax or the qualifications of voters.

Hobby then decided to submit a proposed law which would become known as the open port law. He stressed the fact that the welfare of all the people was the important issue. He asked for a bill that would give the Texas governor the power to keep ports open to commerce by taking full and complete police jurisdiction over areas involved, without the necessity of declaring martial law. The proposed bill further provided that preventing persons from working by threats or violence would be a felony.

The Hobby "open port bill" was actually a forerunner of "right to work" legislation that was to prevail in Texas and other states a quarter of a century later. Then, as in modern times, union officials took vigorous exception to the proposal. One of the Governor's good friends, Representative R. E. Thomason of El Paso, led the opposition.

The legislature not only accepted Hobby's recommendation but went far beyond it to apply it to all operations of common carriers. Violations were made misdemeanors, however, instead of felonies. Hobby was not disappointed at extension of the measure beyond his original concept. He accepted the bill, as passed, with the hope that it would protect the public interest when a breakdown of transportation facilities was threatened. He said that, aside from the material interests of the state, there was ". . . the oldest principle of human liberty, the pursuit of happiness and the inalienable right of every free man to work in any honest and peaceable occupation that he may elect."

The open port law was declared unconstitutional by the Criminal Court of Appeals, but its principles were to be incorporated into laws that would withstand legal challenge.

The Fourth Called Session also created an Industrial Commission, which would investigate and report on controversies between employers and employees when the public welfare might be concerned. The commission would consist of two labor members, two from management and a fifth member selected by the other four to represent the public.

Another important session law was the extension to five years of oil and gas leases on university land, giving leaseholders time to develop their holdings. More than two million acres were involved, and several thousand leases. The act ultimately brought millions of dollars in additional revenue to the state.

One proposition that Will Hobby put forward, and then withdrew because the debate it aroused threatened to prolong the session unduly, later, with modifications became a part of the election code. He had suggested that county executive committees be permitted to have one woman, as well as one man, for each voting precinct, and that a woman, as well as a man, be named to the State Executive Committee from each of the thirty-one senatorial districts.

By merely recommending an investigation into the price of cotton seed, Hobby succeeded in doubling the price in Texas to an average of about forty-five dollars a ton in three days. Discrimination against Texas cotton seed growers had prevailed for years through market manipulations.

The Fourth Called Session proved to be the last under Governor Will Hobby. As in all the legislative sessions of his administration, there had been a minimum of friction and byplay and the passage of many constructive laws.

As the end of Hobby's term approached and he contemplated an orderly transition from his administration to that of the newly-nominated governor, Pat M. Neff, he turned his attention again to a matter that had troubled him since the early days of the World War. Then he had been appalled by the number of prospective soldiers who had to be rejected because of tuberculosis. Now the problem was more acute than ever; many men had contracted the disease during the war or developed it later as the aftermath of poison gas, shell shock or exposure.

Major John C. Townes, the Selective Draft Law administrator, and Dr. C. W. Goddard, the state health officer, shared Governor Hobby's concern over this growing danger. By mid-year 1919 more than 5,000 returned soldiers had been found in need of treatment. Army hospital facilities were insufficient to handle them.

With these three state officials as guiding spirits, the Benevolent War Risk Society was organized, and a committee of distinguished Texans appointed to aid in the movement. A goal of $350,000 in donations was set. By November, 1920, some $150,000 had been raised. Hobby wanted to see the hospital assured before he left office.

With the American Legion backing him, he set November 6 as the date for a one-day statewide drive. The Governor proclaimed it American Legion Memorial Hospital Tag Day, and twenty-four Army Air Service planes from Kelly Field bombarded the state with copies of the proclamation. By nightfall the success of the campaign was assured.

At Hobby's suggestion Senator F. C. Weinert wrote contributors to the drought fund and received their permission to apply repayments to the hospital fund. Captain Charles Schreiner and his son donated a site for the hospital near Kerrville, in the heart of the healthful Hill Country. The little community that grew up around the hospital was named Legion, Texas.

On the national scene it was a time of Republican rejoicing. The country, battle-weary and presumably dubious of Woodrow Wilson's postwar policies, had swung away from the Democratic Party and elected Senator Warren G. Harding of Ohio to the presidency. Texas was honored on November 16, 1920 with a visit from the President-elect. Governor Hobby went to Port Isabel to extend official greetings to the Harding party and to discuss informally the incoming administration's policies toward Mexico.

The meeting was at the home of R. B. Creager, Texas Republican leader. Besides the Governor and his wife, the official Hobby party included Mr. and Mrs. Harry Wiess, Chester Bryan, Robert and Caesar Kleberg of the King Ranch, and Mrs. Hobby's devoted friend, Florence Stratton, of the *Beaumont Enterprise* staff. The President-elect's party included Mrs. Harding and Mrs. Evalyn Walsh McLean, who dazzled her new Texas acquaintances with the famous Hope Diamond.

Mexican problems were real and complicated at that stage of history. The end of the thirty-three-year reign of Porfirio Díaz had been followed by ten years of revolution, counter-revolution and banditry. President Wilson had actually been on the verge of asking for a declaration of war against Mexico during his first term. The unstable Mexican government, the destructive bandit raids on the border, attacks on American citizens in Mexico and, climactically, the accusation that Mexico was pro-German had produced a state of tension on both sides of the Rio Grande.

Hobby had once been an open advocate of American intervention in Mexico. As late as October, 1919, he was saying that only intervention could restore hope, happiness and prosperity to the Mexican people. Such statements caused him to be regarded as an enemy of the Mexican Republic, which definitely was not the case. "It is a question," he said, "of going to the relief of suffering humanity. It is a question of saving women and children who are starving. It is the opening of the door of hope to a people who are helpless and hopeless."

But eventually out of the welter of civil strife and lawlessness had emerged the figure of a strong man who could unite his people and restore order. This man was Álvaro Obregón, from the state of Sonora. He had been a mechanic and became in turn a successful farmer, businessman, industrialist, soldier and political leader.

Now Obregón, after years of determined and sometimes bloody endeavor, was the duly elected president of the Republic of Mexico. Soon he would take the oath of office, ending the provisional regime, headed by his friend Adolfo de la Huerta, which had held sway since their successful revolt against Carranza. The United States, wary of Mexican administrations in general, had not yet recognized the de la Huerta government. For one thing, it was pledged to carry out provisions of the Mexican Constitution of 1917 which contemplated the expropriation of valuable properties held by Americans in Mexico. Both de la Huerta and Obregón insisted that they had no intention of taking title to property without just compensation to American owners, but United States authorities remained skeptical.

Will Hobby had followed closely the ins and outs of Mexican government and, particularly, the program proposed by President-elect Obregón. By the time Obregón crossed the border for a visit, Hobby was convinced of the man's purpose and sincerity.

Hobby went to El Paso to welcome Obregón. At a colorful banquet in honor of the President-to-be, he urged resumption of trade between Mexico and the United States. His was the warmest greeting that a norteamericano had extended to a leader of the turbulent Mexican Republic in years. Only a year after advocating intervention in the same city of El Paso, Hobby was now appealing for recognition of the new regime.

"Mexico has re-won the confidence of the United States," he said. "The old feeling that existed when Texas and Mexico were one has returned. I invite all Mexicans to come to Texas as visitors and friends. We look upon Mexico and the United States as pals in the same great brotherhood of republics."

Hobby invited Obregón to be his guest at the State Fair in Dallas. Obregón was quick to accept and went to Dallas with an entourage of one hundred persons. There Will Hobby made a striking statement that found its way into print around the nation and most of the world.

"May I say to you, General Obregón," the Texas Governor stated, "that as far as Texas is concerned, General Obregón is already recognized."

The President-elect, according to press reports, was visibly moved. He responded with expressions of deep appreciation and a plea for the recognition of the de la Huerta government. He promised to recognize all legal rights and debts of Mexicans and foreigners alike, and to re-establish Mexico's honor and her credit abroad.

On his return to Mexico, Obregón was escorted to the border at El Paso by Adjutant General Cope and Brigadier General Wolters. As a further gesture of good will, Governor Hobby and his own staff accompanied General Jacinto B. Trevino, Mexico's minister of commerce, to the border at Eagle Pass.

Back in Austin, Governor Hobby dispatched a telegram to Woodrow Wilson in the White House urging immediate recognition of the new Mexican government. Washington observers reported the Governor's plea but predicted little would come of it. Within a fortnight Secretary of State Colby proposed the appointment of a joint commission to draft a treaty which could be the basis for resumption of full diplomatic relations between the United States and Mexico.

The news of Colby's proposal found Hobby in Mexico City, attending Obregón's inauguration as the new president's personal and special guest of honor. Pat Neff, the Texas Governor-elect, was also there, and a half-dozen other state governors. But Hobby was the man, next to Obregón, who received the most recognition from the Mexico City press. Photographs and cartoons in the newspapers depicted "our most distinguished visitor, the Governor of Texas."

After ten days in Mexico, Hobby and his party returned to Texas. Newspaper headlines heralded an attempted holdup of the special train by bandits, but the Governor denied any knowledge of it. If anyone tried to hold him up in Mexico, he wasn't aware of it.

The formal recognition of Obregón's government was not to come until 1923. Hobby was no longer governor of Texas then, but the Mexican people had not forgotten that his was one of the first voices raised in Obregón's behalf. It was a long step toward what came to be known as the Good Neighbor Policy.

16

Newspaperman's Administration

INAUGURATION DAY, 1921, marked the first time in years that Texas administrations had changed in the ordinary manner. The incoming governor was Pat Morris Neff, winner over Joe Bailey in the second primary and, of course, triumphant as the Democratic nominee in the general election.

The man spending his last morning in the Governor's Office was William Pettus Hobby. A quiet and reflective man by nature, Will Hobby found these closing hours conducive to thought and recapitulation.

There is always a tinge of sadness in the finish of an administration. The attention of the crowd, of course, focused on the new governor—his staff bustling about, taking charge of everything, whether they knew what to do with it or not—even faithful friends and appointees turning away from the old governor to smile at and wonder about the new . . . and a somehow lonely-looking man, gathering a few papers from the desk, standing back while the adulators pressed forward, finally shaking hands with the man who is now governor and walking out into the corridor, a private citizen.

If Will Hobby had any of these feelings about his own exodus, he concealed them masterfully. He looked and acted like a man anxious to get back to the *Beaumont Enterprise*. As for the Governor's Office, he was glad he had been there and glad he was leaving. The three and a half years just past were years he could remember with justifiable pride. Despite war, drought, pestilence, strikes and hard-hitting political campaigns, they had been years of progress, prosperity, social advancement, political and judicial reform and remarkable strides in public education for Texas.

And they had been years, strangely enough, of unique tranquillity. Hobby's administration had worked in an atmosphere of co-operation. His relations with the legislature, with the press, and with most of his colleagues had been outstandingly cordial. He had been spared much of the censure with which Texans habitually plague their governors. Even some of his most ardent political enemies found, rather to their surprise, that they and Will Hobby were still friends.

When the time came for the outgoing governor to report upon his stewardship to the Thirty-seventh Legislature, he found there was a great deal of constructive history to be read into the record. The contributions of his administration to public education and the highway program were emphasized in his own résumé of his years in office.

One of the aspects of his tenure that he deemed worthy of a special message was his pardon policy. Hobby had drawn some criticism for what some thought was an overliberal attitude on pardons. As a matter of fact, he did exercise the pardoning power (the governor's responsibility alone in that day) quite freely. He conceived it to be as much his duty to give deserving convicts a second chance as it was to see that the underserving paid their debt to society in full.

Hobby's attitude was colored, perhaps, by an experience in the early days of his administration. A Dallas man convicted of an atrocious murder had made a plea for clemency. Friends warned Hobby that it would be a serious political mistake to pardon him. But an investigation by Hobby's staff convinced the Governor that the wrong man had been convicted. He granted the pardon. Later it developed that Hobby had been right; the Dallas man had been falsely accused and convicted.

In explanation of his clemency policy, and perhaps with some compulsion to justify it—although not to apologize for it—Hobby made it the subject of one of his finest legislative messages. It still stands as a powerful statement of a chief executive's most perplexing problem.

"The pardon power is the most difficult of all powers to exercise properly," he said, "because it has its origin not only in the precepts but in the actual performances of the All-Wise Being.

"In the exercise of this function of office, I trust I have been liberal; otherwise, I have fallen short of my aim and my purpose. . . .

"The same Constitution that charges the Governor with the responsibility of enforcing and executing the laws likewise charges him with the responsibility of doing away with or reducing the punishment meted out. . . . The framers of the Constitution did not vest a limited power in the Governor with regard to clemency, but invested him with unlimited power and unqualified discretion to use it. . . .

"In my opinion a person may be justly and promptly convicted of crime and sentenced to the pentitentiary for a term of years, and such person may as truly and thoroughly repent immediately after such conviction, or after serving a brief part of such a sentence, as any length of service may accomplish; and his pardon might restore a good citizen and relieve the State and society of the burden and shame of one more convict, and return one more good citizen to the support and care of a needy and unprotected family, and give to him and to them an opportunity to rebuild a good home and a good name. When I have reached such a conclusion in a given case, I have not hesitated to execute the mandate of the Constitution and give the convict a chance to demonstrate his worthiness of the pardoning power.

"In trying to determine each individual case, I am not ashamed to admit that I have never been unmindful of the splendid example of the Master who graciously and fully pardoned the repentant thief on the Cross, and I think that example worthy of the whole world's emulation.

"I have doubtless made mistakes in withholding it, but when the people conferred this power on the Governor, they knew some mistakes would be made because no human could unerringly exercise it. . . . My only regret is not in liberating any of those whom I have liberated, but that lack of time, knowledge of facts, or any other circumstances should have caused me to make the mistake of not liberating those, if any there be, who should have been liberated."

(Fifteen years later the constitution would be amended to dilute the governor's pardoning power by creating a Board of Pardons and Paroles which had to recommend clemency before the governor could grant it. And almost two decades after that, the State of Texas would put into effect a probation law that permitted trial judges to keep out of prison those persons who, presumably, had "truly and thoroughly repent [ed] immediately after such conviction. . . .")

Hobby's last pardon was granted under circumstances he would always remember with wry amusement. It was after dark on Saturday evening, before Neff's inauguration scheduled for the following Tuesday, when Governor Hobby closed his office door and started out through the dimly lighted corridor. From behind a giant pillar, a man stepped out and confronted him.

"Governor Hobby, I need to talk to you," he said in an agitated manner. Hobby correctly interpreted the man's tension.

"I'd be glad to talk with you," the Governor replied, "but if it is about a pardon, I'll have to tell you that it is too late. I am not going to grant any more pardons. I will be governor for only two more days; the new man will be governor for at least two years. You'll have to see him about it."

The stranger said slowly: "Yes, I did want to see you about a pardon for my brother. I know you have only two more days in office. But I have an idea you can do me more good in two days than the new man can in two years."

Intrigued by the candor of this approach, Hobby looked up the brother's record, found it acceptable and granted the pardon. As for the visitor's premonition about Governor Neff, it proved to be valid. Neff's pardon policy was to be much more strict than Hobby's had been.

When the hour arrived for Hobby's final address to the legislature, he remained true to character. He said much had been accomplished while he was governor, and told what it was, and gave the credit to the legislature and to his friends and advisers.

Unusually large balances were left to the credit of every state department, he reported, and the largest sum to that date in the permanent school fund. At the same time he was able to point to vast improvements in the school system, the virtual doubling of the per capita apportionment and the reduction of the ad valorem tax rate from thirty-five to twenty-two cents per hundred-dollar valuation. The Highway Department had been activated and expanded; county road aid had been quadrupled; state highway mileage had been more than doubled. Because of the rise in oil and gas production and the levying of the first production taxes on petroleum, all this and more had been accomplished without other new or additional taxes.

Most Texas newspapers marked the close of the "newspaperman's administration" with commendatory editorials. One of the best summaries was Colonel George Bailey's, in the *Houston Post*:

"There has been nothing spectacular about William P. Hobby in either his public or private career. From his youth up he has belonged in the category of quiet, serious-minded, diligent and modest persons who are always striving to achieve their objectives. If as a journalist Hobby had possessed the egotism of Hearst or as a statesman he were imbued with the audacity so common in the average individual who so classifies himself, the Hobby administration would not be permitted to expire quietly.

"But Hobby, being neither bold nor brilliant nor blatant, merely sends to the legislature a brief résumé of the outstanding achievements of his administration as if his three years of tenure were uneventful and his official acts and utterances entirely commonplace.

"Yet judged by results and judged fairly, the Hobby administration has been the most remarkable in many respects in the history of Texas, and it has been remarkable for the most part because of Hobby himself.

"Be it remembered that Hobby came into the governorship under peculiarly distressing circumstances. The *Post* will not recount them here further than to say that circumstances surrounding Hobby had much hostility. The personnel with whom he had to co-operate was not of his choosing, and he encountered from that source not a little animosity and resentment. From within, envenomed men sought at the beginning to discredit him and defeat his purpose.

"But plodding along in his quiet way, he soon marked out a line of policy, and very soon he was showing the people that they had a governor who was on the job, even though he might not be the governor of their choosing.

"Speaking briefly, Hobby proved a helpful friend to the university in its most serious crisis. Then, to use his own words, he devoted all his endeavors to making Texas as useful as possible in the supreme task of winning the war. The Zone Law, so-called, will live as the decisive blow that as a war measure, destroyed the saloon in Texas. It was Hobby's idea, and Hobby was a lifelong antiprohibitionist.

"No state boasted a more efficient or more effective war governor.

"But the outstanding feature of the Hobby administration must ever remain the progress of common school education under the impulse of the Hobby policies. The school terms of the rural schools have been lengthened, the salaries of the teachers have been increased, rendering certain higher standards in the teaching force in the state, and Texas is at last on the way to enjoy a gratifying rank among the states with respect to public education.

"It has cost considerable money to bring about this condition but Hobby had the courage to take the lead, believing it necessary for the welfare of the state. What Hobby achieved could have been done ten years ago, twenty years ago or forty years ago just as well, but former governors and legislatures

Oveta Culp Hobby, President Eisenhower, Will Hobby—photograph taken in 1955 when Mrs. Hobby was Secretary of Health, Education, and Welfare.

The Hobby Family in the Houston home of Governor and
Mrs. Hobby in 1958. Seated: William P. Hobby and Oveta
Culp Hobby. Standing (*left to right*): Bill Hobby, Jr., his
wife Diana Poteat Hobby, Henry Catto, Jessica Hobby Catto.

were not quite prepared to risk such expenditures. To jump the per capita of expenditures per scholastic from $7.50 to $14.50 in three years required real courage, but Hobby met the test and has shown us that many of our elder statesmen were wrong in believing the people were opposed to taxation for the improvement of the common school system.

"If Hobby had accomplished nothing else of importance, what he did for public education—higher and common school and eleemosynary—would make his administration notable. But his entire administration was marked by similar intelligent treatment of problems and emergencies, which were constantly arising as a result of the war. And of the postbellum period, the open port policy and the right-to-work law will stand the test, we think, as a piece of constructive statesmanship of the highest order.

"The *Post* takes occasion to remark these features of the Hobby administration, because of the unreasonable, even absurd criticism to which thoughtless men have subjected the retiring Governor. He does not need the *Post's* defense. He has always been able to fight his own battles, and the *Post* does not hesitate to say that it thinks he has made some mistakes.

"But the mistakes were trivial compared with the big things which remained as brighter achievements, and the *Post* believes the intelligent, fair-minded student of Texas history must inevitably reach the conclusion that, all things considered, no preceding administration achieved in so great degree for the permanent welfare and progress of the commonwealth."

This was the evaluation of Hobby's administration through the friendly but candid eye of a former associate. The comments of Ferguson and Bailey fanatics, antiprohibitionists (even though Hobby himself was one), antisuffragettes, some labor leaders rankling under the Hobby right-to-work law, and even some open-shop organizers who resented his expressions of fairness toward labor, were less realistic, perhaps, and certainly less complimentary.

As for the *Post's* attitude that Hobby had made "some mistakes," Hobby himself thoroughly agreed. Any conscientious man who was not a complete egotist, having faced the multitudinous duties and decisions of the Governor's Office, would admit occasional blunders.

Some weeks after Neff's inauguration Hobby dropped into the executive offices to pay his respects to the Governor. He found Neff up to his handsome aquiline nose in work; Neff's desk was piled high with papers and he was visibly harassed by problems of the day.

"Governor," said Neff jokingly, and yet with a trace of the querulous in his tone, "I understand that you used to find time, on occasion, to take the afternoon off from this job and play golf. I want to know how you did it."

"Well, Governor," Hobby said with a twinkle in his eye, "after you have been here a little while longer, you will find as I did that if you work just half a day, you will make only half as many mistakes as when you work all day."

Will Hobby went home to Beaumont with no regrets, and with a growing eagerness to get back in the publisher's seat at the *Enterprise*, back to the business of building a newspaper and a city. He never thought of himself as a professional politician. He had learned much in his seven years at Austin; the experience would prove invaluable to him down the road. He had answered a call to public service and had done his best under trying circumstances; he had won the respect of those who watch the practices of statecraft with a discerning eye—and he had earned, for the rest of his life, the dignified and honorable title of "Governor."

The office of governor in Texas may be short on constitutional authority, but it is long on prestige and recognition. Most people are as impressed by a governor as the Negro minister who, by special invitation, conducted a marriage ceremony for the Hobbys' maid and a capitol porter in the Mansion. After exacting the necessary vows, he concluded, "And now, in the presence of the Governor of Texas and God Almighty, I pronounce you man and wife."

17

Rehitched to the Post

WILL HOBBY (still "Governor" to his friends) found that Beaumont had doubled in population during his absence. The once-sleepy sawmill town was now a thriving seaport of 40,000 souls. Oil, rice and lumber were still the staples of its commerce, but there were opportunities for growth in all directions. And the *Enterprise* had grown with Beaumont. Jim Mapes had done his work well.

At first the old routine was exhilarating. Hobby resumed his editorial exhortations from the text of industrial and civic development. He applauded the Beaumont Temperance Club when, finding itself at least temporarily without a cause, it donated its fine four-story building for a city hall. He started a campaign to deepen the Sabine-Neches Waterway to thirty feet. Within a year that was done. Things were the same as ever, except there were more of them and they moved faster.

Hobby said that, some day, Beaumont might rival Houston. He even dreamed aloud of the day when Beaumont and Port Arthur, less than twenty miles to the south, might join their boundaries and merge into a great metropolis.

The *Enterprise's* afternoon competitor, the *Beamont Journal,* was making itself felt since joining the Marsh-Fentress chain, which also operated newspapers in Austin and Waco. Hobby solved that problem with direct action: he bought the *Journal.*

With both a morning and an evening newspaper on his hands, he entered upon what was then considered the daring experiment of publishing separate and competing newspapers under a single management under the same roof. From the physical and managerial viewpoints, the two papers were one. Editorially, they retained their respective identities, and their staffs were encouraged to compete quite as fiercely as when they were blood enemies instead of stepbrothers. The editor-in-chief, who was to co-ordinate the news-gathering and spreading operation, was Alfred Jones, the young man Hobby had hired from the defunct *Houston Telegram*.

In the middle of the negotiations that made Hobby a twenty-four-hour-a-day publisher, he was called to his mother's bedside in Dallas. She died a few days after he arrived. Will's fondness for his mother had been enhanced during the years since Captain Edwin Hobby's death in 1899.

Incidentally, it was through his mother's side of the family that the impetus came for a unique distinction for Will Hobby. A village near the IGN Railroad in eastern Fort Bend County was named Hobby in his honor. Contributing to the choice of name was the fact that Hobby's maternal grandfather, Dr. John Pettus, had settled in Fort Bend County in 1858. Hobby was a one-store city, but it gave Will the distinction of being the only modern Texas governor with a town for a namesake.

Back in Beaumont after his mother's passing, Hobby became conscious of a gradual change in his feeling toward his own contribution to his newspapers. It was not so much a dissatisfied as an unsatisfied feeling. Quite likely it was a matter of a vigorous and successful businessman in the prime of life looking around for new worlds to conquer.

The "combination" experiment was working out well for the *Enterprise* and the *Journal;* in fact, it was to lead to other morning-evening combinations in Fort Worth, Galveston, Austin, Waco, Wichita Falls, San Angelo, Corpus Christi, Lubbock, Amarillo and other cities in and out of Texas. The circulation and revenues of the newspapers had been pushed about as fast and as far as the size and resources of Beaumont warranted. And a man couldn't spend the rest of his life deepening the Sabine-Neches Waterway channel.

Hobby looked up Jim Mapes and gave him a surprising bit of news: he, Will Hobby, was going back to Houston.

He would retain his interest in the *Enterprise* and *Journal,* but Mapes would run them. Mapes had proved he could do that and agreed to continue, although he would be sorry to see Hobby leave Beaumont. (Mapes later acquired Hobby's interest in the *Enterprise* and *Journal*)

So it was that in mid-1922 Governor Hobby came back home to Houston. He had many friends there, old and new, who welcomed his return. He was in no hurry to make a business connection; he wanted to take a long-needed rest and look around awhile.

Houston was a city worth looking at. The rough village started by the Allen brothers on Buffalo Bayou in 1836 was now about to become the largest city in Texas and the second largest in the South. Houston's manmade ship channel brought the world's goods to its docks and carried away oil, cotton, rice, sugar, beef and all the other products of Southeast Texas fields, ranges, factories and rich mineral deposits. Its broad streets were becoming canyons of commerce as stores and banks expanded and high-rising office buildings pushed up the skyline.

Houston had everything—industry, transportation, raw materials, venture capital, elbow room, people in ever-increasing numbers, and dynamic leadership. The distinguished former governor, a successful man in his own right, took his proper place with such men as Jesse Jones, Will Clayton, John T. Scott, Jim West, John Henry Kirby, Captain Baker, Joe and Will Rice, R. L. Blaffer, Harry Wiess, C. L. Carter, Joe S. Cullinan, Joe Evans, Ross Sterling, Howard Hughes, Tom Ball, Camille Pillot, Captain Hutcheson, H. M. Garwood, Mike and Will Hogg, and dozens of other leaders of comparable stature.

Will Hobby, who had come to rest and look around Houston, probably did more of the latter. One of the local points of greatest interest to him was his old newspaper, the *Houston Post*. He found its current demeanor intriguing but somewhat puzzling. There was also an interesting rumor that the *Post*, in spite of its recent growth, was less prosperous than formerly.

Young Roy Watson had taken over the *Post* from the old triumvirate of Rienzi Johnston, G. J. Palmer and H. F. MacGregor. As the late J. L. Watson had intended, they ran the paper for twenty years until his son was twenty-five. Young Watson became president on May 28, 1917, moving Johnston to chairman of the board and editor-in-chief.

Not many months passed before both Johnston and Palmer were forced into retirement, albeit under generous annuity arrangements. Roy Watson was a handsome, blond, idealistic young man, a Princeton graduate whose years had been spent in North Carolina, New York and Chicago. Before moving to Houston in 1914, he had been in the city only once. Personally he was well liked by the *Post* family; he brought back his father's sunny, friendly personality and forthright character.

As for his newspapering, that was another matter, and one about which the old-timers were dubious. Watson found the *Post's* previous attitudes and policies almost wholly distasteful. He made a clean sweep of the incumbents in key jobs and quickly turned the *Post* into an anti-saloon, pro-suffragette, pro-Woodrow Wilson and anti-Joe Bailey sheet. The shock was almost too much, for staff and readers alike.

The Watson ethics caused as great a revolution in the business office as in the editorial room. He banned from the *Post's* columns all wildcat oil stock, liquor, wine and beer advertising. Then he extended the ban to patent medicine advertising, including yeast. Warned that his edicts would cost the *Post* $90,000 a year, Watson said that was the equivalent of purchasing a $90,000 feature called principle.

Watson held daily conferences with his department heads, with the group going over each day's work in each department. The erudite Colonel George Bailey writhed in pain as the heads of the business and mechanical departments criticized his editorials.

Ross Sterling, one of the founders and president of the Humble Oil and Refining Company, had tried several times to buy the *Post*. An ambassador representing William Randolph Hearst tentatively offered Watson some $1,150,000 for the paper. But Watson publicly announced: "The *Post* is not for sale, never has been for sale, and never will be for sale."

Sterling turned in another direction for the daily newspaper he had his heart set on. He had recently resigned as Humble president and sold his stock for $8,000,000. The talk around Houston was that he wanted to run for governor and needed a newspaper to serve as a mouthpiece for his opinions on public affairs. Sterling started pouring money into a new competitor of the *Post,* a daily called the *Dispatch*.

The *Dispatch* had a healthy circulation but sold almost no advertising, mainly because of a charge (always denied) that it had been started as an organ of the Ku Klux Klan. Sterling put more than $400,000 into the *Dispatch* within a few months. He bought the finest features and ordered that no expense be spared in making it Houston's best daily.

One day in mid-July, 1922, Roy Watson called Sterling, and the two met in Watson's elaborate office. To Sterling's astonishment, Watson calmly announced that he was ready to sell the *Post*. He said Sterling could have it for the same price Hearst was reputedly willing to pay.

Sterling quickly accepted. He wrote out a check for the down payment and agreed to pay the balance in six months. Then he called Will Hobby.

Would Hobby become president of the combined *Post* and *Dispatch?* It took Hobby approximately as long to agree to that proposal as it had for Sterling to grab Watson's offer.

Roy Watson explained his change of heart this way: "Without volition on my part my mental attitude changed, and while I had no particular desire to sell the paper, I felt that

I would be willing to sell if a good enough offer came along. I consider $1,150,000 good enough. Incidentally, the afternoon of the day Mr. Sterling agreed to the purchase, I received a telegram from Mr. Hearst inviting me to his West Coast offices to close the deal I had talked over with his representative."

This was the opportunity Will Hobby had been waiting for, consciously or not, since he had come back to Houston. On August 1 appeared the first issue of the *Houston Post-Dispatch*, with Hobby as a stockholder, director and president. The wide-eyed boy from the Big Thicket country was running the newspaper on which he had started his career as an eight-dollar-a-week circulation clerk.

The first issue carried this message from him:

> *"The makers of the* Houston Post-Dispatch *feel the ardor and the zeal which comes with a new opportunity for service. Two newspapers, drawing support from the same people, bound by the ties of loyalty to the same public welfare, have joined together.*
>
> *"The object and purpose is to make it possible for Houston to have one morning newspaper measuring up to the best standards of journalism of the best American cities, keeping step with Houston's progress, helping every cause that is good. We can accomplish this end only by having the good will and co-operation of all, not a part, but all of the good people of Houston. We appreciate the kind words of the* Chronicle *and the* Press *already. We hope to be useful to our constituents and only their aid will enable us to do what we are here to do.*
>
> *"W. P. Hobby, President."*

Hobby enjoyed his reunion with old friends and former co-workers such as Colonel Bailey and Judd Mortimer Lewis. The general manager was Ray Dudley, an old friend of Ross Sterling. The managing editor was Charlie Maes, who had been "Watsonized" from the city editorship of the *Post* and joined Sterling's *Dispatch* after a term with the *Chronicle*.

Below the masthead of the paper was this box: "The *Houston Post-Dispatch,* an independent newspaper, printing the news impartially, supporting what it believes to be right and opposing what it believes to be wrong without regard to partisan politics."

This pronouncement of independence from political party discipline soon had its first test. In the hot Democratic run-off for governor in 1924 the *Post-Dispatch* supported neither the Klan-sponsored Felix Robertson nor Mrs. Miriam A. Ferguson, wife of the former governor. Mrs. Ferguson won the nomination by nearly 100,000 votes.

In the general election her Republican opponent was Dr. George Butte, the University of Texas law professor whose services Hobby had enlisted to write important oil, gas, pipeline and gas utilities regulations for the Railroad Commission. The *Post-Dispatch* created a ripple of excitement, and some consternation, by announcing that it would support Dr. Butte.

Will Hobby had been a "regular Democrat" all his life. He may have suffered some qualms about backing a Republican candidate for governor in Democratic Texas; if so, he kept them to himself. Ross Sterling, owner of the *Post-Dispatch,* abominated the name of Ferguson.

Neither Sterling nor Hobby thought Butte had any chance to win. The *Post-Dispatch* admitted as much editorially.

"His candidacy, however, sounds a note of lofty idealism that is not often heard in latter-day politics," the editorial commented.

The *Houston Chronicle,* still headed by Hobby's old friend Marcellus E. Foster, criticized its competitor for bolting the Democratic ticket. The *Post-Dispatch* countered by printing a facsimile of a 1922 *Chronicle* editorial saying that citizenship was higher than the party pledge.

"Many will vote for Ma Ferguson," the *Post-Dispatch* said, "but no one, not even the editor of the *Chronicle,* will vote for her because he thinks she is more capable than Dr. Butte."

Actually, the race was closer than expected. Mrs. Ferguson

was elected, 422,558 to 294,970, and there was some speculation that Dr. Butte would have done considerably better if more people had realized his strength.

A Ferguson was back in the Governor's Office, but Ross Sterling's *Post-Dispatch* regularly reminded Farmer Jim that his wife's election should not be taken as condonement of the acts for which he had been removed from office.

Business matters, more than politics, were occupying Will Hobby's attention. There was the suit filed by the Pulitzer Publishing Company of St. Louis seeking to restrain the Houston company from using the name "Post-Dispatch," which it regarded as the exclusive property of its own newspaper of the same name. There was the chore of moving the *Post-Dispatch* plant from the old building at Texas Avenue and Travis Street to more spacious quarters at Polk and Dowling, which was out of the crowded business center of Houston. Sterling soon started a new *Post-Dispatch* building. And then there was the important matter of going into radio broadcasting business.

Hobby and Walter Sterling had convinced the senior Sterling that it would be both a public service and sound business to enter radio. The new medium was not yet a serious competitor of the newspaper for advertising revenues, but Hobby foresaw that it might well become one in short order. By getting in early, the *Post-Dispatch* could purchase a station with a small amount of capital. Waiting would invite the development of a strong competing medium and force the price up.

Hobby preferred to see Houston radio grow up as a partner of his newspaper, not as a rival. He had already recognized the public interest in radio by starting, on February 22, 1925, a radio page in the Sunday edition.

Late in April, Sterling came to terms with Will Horowitz, a local theater man who owned a station, and on May 9 dedication ceremonies marked the opening of Station KPRC in its studios on the roof of the *Post-Dispatch* building. Among the first speakers were Mayor Oscar Holcombe, General

Manager Ray Dudley, Judd Mortimer Lewis and, of course, Will Hobby.

To create an audience for the radio station and, at the same time, increase its own circulation, the *Post-Dispatch* offered a package deal: for $6, a six-months' subscription and a crystal receiving set. It was a popular proposition and thousands of sets were sold. Incidentally, the sets had an attractive feature, from the *Post-Dispatch's* viewpoint: KPRC was the only station they could receive.

The *Post-Dispatch* and Ross Sterling got another opportunity to oppose "Fergusonism" in 1926, and this time with success. Fiery Dan Moody, who had been elected attorney general on the strength of his prosecutions of Ku Klux Klan leaders while he was serving as a district attorney, was running against Mrs. Ferguson. Alleged scandals in the Highway Commission had weakened her support and Moody almost won over the field in the first primary.

The Governor had been quoted as saying she would withdraw if Moody led the ticket. After the primary, however, she said that the statement had been made by her husband, not herself, and she was staying in the run-off.

The *Post-Dispatch,* early and late, had assured its subscribers that "Dan's the Man." Moody won by a landslide.

Early in his administration Governor Moody selected Ross Sterling as chairman of the embattled Highway Commission. Sterling announced that he would give his full time to the Highway Department, which meant that Will Hobby would be left virtually in charge of the Houston newspaper and the radio station. As Hobby was still publisher of the *Beaumont Enterprise-Journal,* he now occupied a position of unparalleled influence in Texas newspaperdom—the control and direction of three metropolitan dailies and a radio outlet.

While it was a period of increasing prestige and personal satisfaction for the former governor, it also brought him personal heartaches. Back in February of 1926, near the close of an unusually cold winter, death had come to Rienzi Melville Johnston. Will Hobby owed much to this sagacious, able newspaperman and political seer. Johnston had been mentor and faithful friend for thirty years.

In 1927 two more blows fell. In February, Colonel George Bailey, vice president and editor of the *Post-Dispatch*, a writer and a man whom Hobby vastly admired, died. And in November Edwin Hobby died suddenly in Kerrville.

Edwin and Will Hobby had been as close as it is possible for brothers to be. In all of Will's important decisions Edwin's advice had been sought and almost invariably followed. It was Edwin who encouraged him to enter politics. The unexpected death of his brother plunged Will Hobby even deeper into the day-by-day routine of newspaper-making as therapy for shock.

This was the year that floods on the Mississippi left 75,000 homeless and concentrated national attention on flood control; that Lindbergh flew the Atlantic alone; that Silent Cal Coolidge announced he "did not choose to run" for another term as President. The prospect of an open fight for the presidency in 1928 added zest and importance to preparations for the nominating conventions. The man selected by the Democrats might well become President—and that man was going to be selected right in Houston, Texas.

18

Political Patterns

JESSE JONES, a big man physically, financially and civically in booming Houston, made big news on January 12, 1928. The official announcement came that Houston would be the site of the Democratic National Convention. Jones, as party finance chairman since 1924, had pulled important strings. It would be the first major party convention in the South since the ill-starred Democratic convention at Charleston in 1860.

The convention was scheduled for mid-June. It would bring more than 25,000 delegates, visitors and correspondents to Houston. Houston had five months in which to get ready. The resulting activity was phenomenal, even for Houston and Jesse Jones.

In ten days a committee raised $350,000 for expenses. Jones put up a six-story Democratic Building for a headquarters. Sam Houston Hall, designed to fit the convention's needs for a meeting place, was completed in sixty-four days at a cost of $200,000. Two special "hospitality houses" were built to accommodate the expected overflow. Over $2,000,000 in bonds were sold for city improvements.

As Jones pushed and pulled Houston into a state of preparedness, he found that one of his most energetic and effective co-workers was Will Hobby, the president of the *Post-Dispatch*. The two men were acquainted, of course, but this was their first close association. Out of it came a lasting friendship built on mutual regard and appreciation.

Principal contenders for the Democratic nomination were Governor Al Smith of New York and Senator James A. Reed of Missouri. Smith seemed to be forging into a commanding position, despite his weakness in the "Solid South," where there was considerable resistance to the selection of a candidate who was a Northerner, a "wet," a Roman Catholic and a protégé of Tammany Hall. In fact, Jones's bid to bring the convention to Houston had been abetted by Smith backers who thought Southerners might be mollified by the gesture.

Of Smith's handicaps in Texas, the most serious was his well-known opposition to prohibition. Most of the pre-convention backing, filling and haggling among Texas Democrats was in an attempt to reconcile the old wet and dry forces so as to present a united front.

The *Post-Dispatch* once suggested that "Dry Dan Moody would make an ideal running mate for moist Al Smith." Governor Moody disturbed Will Hobby and other "moderators" when he publicly stated he was opposed to a "wet" candidate for president. A few days later the Governor softened the declaration by saying he would support the party nominee, wet or dry, but would work diligently for a dry plank in the platform.

Out of the Governor's stand, with the help of prominent party leaders including Hobby and M. M. Crane, came a proposal known as the "Moody Plan." It was to send the Texas delegation to the convention unpledged to any candidate but committed to work for a platform plank supporting the 18th Amendment, opposing repeal and urging vigorous enforcement of prohibition laws. Later the *Post-Dispatch* suggested an alternate plan of instructing the state delegation for native son Jesse Jones. A harmony group which called itself the "Democrats of Texas," headed by former Lieutenant Governor Lynch Davidson with Hobby as first vice-president, had Moody's support, but there was a limit to compromise. On May 2 the red-headed Governor told 4,000 Houstonians:

"If Al Smith is nominated for president, the State of Texas is not going to be responsible."

Bone-dry opposition to the "Moody Plan" developed in a "Constitutional Democrats" group with Senator Tom Love as its leader. A *Post-Dispatch* story on May 16 quoted Steve Pinckney, of the Davidson-Hobby crowd, as saying that the Constitutional Democrats were "a gang of Ku Kluxers."

A week before the state convention in Beaumont, in late May, the *Post-Dispatch* quoted Dan Moody as suggesting that the Texas delegation be instructed to vote for Jesse Jones as the presidential nominee, to avoid a factional fight. And that, after much tumult and shouting, was what the Beaumont convention decided to do.

It was a hard-won clear-cut victory for "harmony" and the Moody forces, with an anti-Smith delegation under Moody's control pledged to support Jones for the nomination.

Colonel Tom Ball, the old champion of Texas prohibitionists, made the nominating speech for Jesse Jones at the National Convention. Al Smith's name was put up in a spirited speech by the Democratic vice-presidential candidate of 1920, Franklin Delano Roosevelt. Half a dozen other Texas favorite sons were nominated, along with Congressman Cordell Hull of Tennessee and U. S. Senators Reed of Missouri, Alben Barkley of Kentucky, Walter George of Georgia and G. M. Hitchcock of Nebraska. Smith was nominated on the first ballot, with Texas' forty votes going to Jones.

As a sop to the South, the convention nominated Senator Joseph T. Robinson of Arkansas for vice-president. Texans thought Dan Moody or Jesse Jones would have been a stronger running mate for the "Happy Warrior."

The Convention closed in Sam Houston Hall with rumblings of an approaching storm already audible in the wings. Al Smith's acceptance telegram promised "fundamental changes" in the prohibition laws. Sixteen Southern states had already voiced opposition to the nomination of any candidate not fully committed to complete prohibition. The Democratic Party was headed for a wide-open split.

Hobby and the *Post-Dispatch* turned manfully to the uphill task of holding Texas Democrats in line for the nominees. They also busied themselves with the important tasks of helping to re-elect Moody as governor and carry Ross Sterling's proposed statewide highway construction bond issue.

In the heat of the battle Hobby was plagued by an awkward local situation. Sterling had pledged his support to Walter Woodul for the state senate; now Will Hobby's lifelong family friend and supporter John Henry Kirby announced against Woodul. It was not easy for Hobby to oppose Kirby; the *Post-Dispatch* said that, while it was supporting Woodul, it would say nothing to the detriment of Mr. Kirby. Happily, Kirby withdrew before the second primary and rescued Hobby from his uncomfortable position.

The September state party convention, although still heavy with anti-Smith sentiment and even including some delegates who wanted to vote for Herbert Hoover, resulted in another victory for the "harmony" forces led by Moody, Jones and Hobby. The Democratic organization was supplemented by a "Smith-Robinson League of First Voters," with Miss Oveta Culp of Killeen and Houston as state chairman. Miss Culp had been parliamentarian of the Texas House of Representatives and executive secretary of the Women's Democratic League at Houston.

It was not, however, a year for harmony on the Texas front. The general election in November gave the Republican ticket its first victory in the Lone Star State. The *Post-Dispatch* had to report grimly that even its home county of Harris had gone for Hoover. The only consolation, it said, was that "the vote in Texas gives striking confirmation to the belief that this state will be, from now on out, a battleground in presidential elections." The prophecy would have to wait twenty-four years for fulfillment.

Over the years the legend was to grow that Al Smith lost Texas because he was a Roman Catholic. Undoubtedly the element of religious prejudice did exist, but contemporary observers were generally convinced that prohibition was the most damaging issue.

After its national disaster, the *Post-Dispatch* had better luck on the home front. Houston's energetic and ambitious young mayor, Oscar Holcombe, had sponsored some progressive measures that received the *Post-Dispatch's* approbation, but he had run afoul of its criticism on some other scores. In the December election the paper endorsed Walter Monteith over Holcombe, and Monteith was elected. This was not the last, of course, that the *Post-Dispatch* and Houston would hear of Oscar Holcombe. With a few intermissions he would be the chief figure in city government well past the mid-century mark.

Ross Sterling, meanwhile, was doing an outstanding job as chairman of the State Highway Commission. Late in the year, when he and Hobby were both honor guests for the opening of the South Texas State Fair at Beaumont, Hobby dropped a well-timed bombshell on the Texas political landscape. In the course of a brief speech he remarked that the audience might not realize it was beholding, in himself and the Highway Commission chairman, "one governor in retrospect and another in prospect." It was the first prominent mention of Sterling as a gubernatorial possibility, and the wire services obligingly spread the statement far and wide.

Politics and the publishing business faded out of Will Hobby's mind with the shock of a grievous personal loss. On January 15, 1929, death came suddenly to his wife of fourteen years, Willie Cooper Hobby.

The helpmate of his difficult Austin years and the period of expansion in Beaumont and Houston, Willie had also provided a close tie with Will Hobby's beginnings in the sawmill country of Deep East Texas. Her father, the late ex-Congressman Bronson Cooper, although born in Kentucky, had been brought by his parents to Woodville, Tyler County, when he was less than a year old. His first law firm was that of Nicks, Hobby and Cooper, and later for a period he had been a partner of John Henry Kirby. When Will Hobby was a young publisher in Beaumont, he and Congressman Cooper worked closely in the early stages of waterway development that eventually brought realization of Beaumont's long dream of deep water.

In April occurred another death that touched Hobby deeply. Joseph Weldon Bailey died while taking part in a law case at Sherman. The redoubtable Senator Bailey had been a warm friend and both a political ally and rival of Will Hobby, who wrote in the *Post-Dispatch:*

"He was distinguished, not only for his ability, but for his sincerity and courage. To me his death brings . . . a keen sense of personal loss."

One of the worst floods in Houston's history, in June, caused tremendous property loss along Buffalo Bayou and set off an effort to secure tax remissions to Harris County for flood control. Hobby had a major part in the project. In October he was a delegate to the Intra-Coastal Canal Association convention in Beaumont and spoke at the dedication of a new highway from Corpus Christi to the Rio Grande Valley. Again he hinted that the gentleman on the platform with him, Highway Chairman Ross Sterling, might well be the next governor of Texas.

On May 30, 1930, Hobby's forecast moved a long step toward realization. Ross S. Sterling announced that he would run for governor.

The *Post-Dispatch* commented in its "Houston" column: "In view of the fact that its publisher, R. S. Sterling, has entered the Democratic primaries as a candidate for governor, the *Post-Dispatch* deems it appropriate to make a fresh statement of policy as follows:

"References made in this column or on the editorial page to Mr. Sterling's candidacy will be confined for the most part to quotations expressing the viewpoints of others.

"The *Post-Dispatch* will not deviate from its fixed policy of treating all candidacies fairly and according them space within reasonable limits to express their ideas on public questions."

Before the campaigns of 1930 could get up steam, the State Democratic Executive Committee had to settle with the "Hoovercrats." Party extremists were demanding that those who had bolted the party in 1928 be barred from the Democratic primaries. The *Post-Dispatch* urged against such a drastic course, and the committee concurred. It was decided, however, that "Hoovercrats" could not run for any office in the Democratic primaries.

Sterling's entry matched him with Mrs. Miriam A. Ferguson, seeking her second term after the four-year tenure of Dan Moody. It was an eleven-candidate field which included, as other prominent contenders, Lieutenant Governor Barry Miller, Earle B. Mayfield, the "dry" bellwether Tom Love and State Senator Clint C. Small. Mrs. Ferguson led in the first primary by some 72,000 votes, with Sterling making the run-off by 32,000 votes over Senator Small.

The second primary brought all the anti-Ferguson forces to Sterling's aid and he was nominated by a 90,000-vote margin.

As Sterling took the oath of office in January of 1931, Texas was beginning to suffer in earnest from the Great Depression. Moreover, an oil boom in East Texas was threatening literally to drown out the market and create economic and political problems of disastrous proportions. Ross Sterling had been ambitious, for some years, to be governor of Texas. He could hardly have chosen a worse time.

19

The Hobby Team

The *Post-Dispatch* society page of February 15, 1931, mentioned in a rather offhand manner that a wedding of interest to Houstonians was about to take place in Temple. Mr. and Mrs. I. W. Culp were announcing the approaching marriage of their daughter Oveta to the former governor of Texas, William Pettus Hobby. On February 23, in a simple ceremony at the Culp residence, Oveta and Will were married.

The bride was by no means unknown in Houston. She had achieved statewide notice in 1927 when Speaker Robert Lee Bobbitt appointed her parliamentarian of the house when she was barely old enough to vote. Her work with young voters in the 1928 presidential campaign had brought further recognition. The following year she had become assistant to Houston City Attorney John H. Freeman. In 1930 she had run an unsuccessful but close race for the legislature from Harris County.

Young, bright and attractive, Oveta Culp Hobby was marked for leadership in what was generally considered a man's world of politics and business and in other spheres not yet in prospect.

Oveta's ripening friendship with Will Hobby had been a recent thing, but the name of Hobby has long been in her mind—and with a distinctly unfavorable connotation. In later years she often recalled with merriment the first time she ever heard of Will Hobby. She said she could still see her mother, dressed in the height of 1918 fashion, standing in the door of their Killeen home, drawing on her long white gloves and calling back to Oveta and her sister, "You'll have to can the peaches, girls; I'm going out to campaign for Will Hobby."

The Culp sisters spent many hot summer hours picking, peeling and canning enormous quantities of peaches, with appropriate side comments about Will Hobby, whoever he was.

The formation of the Hobby "team," which was to accomplish many remarkable things in publishing, politics and civic progress, came at a time when Will most needed Oveta's understanding and companionship. The depression had already struck a heavy blow at his personal fortunes. A few years before he had acquired an interest in an insurance business with George Christie, and the company had expanded rapidly. The financial recession that followed the stock market crash of 1929 brought disaster to Hobby's insurance holdings. The company had gone into receivership, with heavy losses for both policyholders and stockholders. At the time of his marriage it was in debt almost $200,000 on obligations for which Hobby felt personally responsible.

The insurance collapse represented the greatest trial and embarrassment of Will Hobby's life. It took years, but with Oveta's help he worked out of it.

Meanwhile the depression was making inroads even on as sound a business as the *Post-Dispatch*. Circulation was going down, for the first time since the old *Post* was launched in 1885. True, Hobby and Sterling had doubled the list of subscribers since taking over in 1924. But now the trend was downward, and Hobby correctly reckoned that it was a sign of trouble ahead.

Houston was still one of the more prosperous centers of the country, and the *Post-Dispatch* lost no opportunity to point with pride to that fact. Houston bank deposits in 1931 were $160,000,000, compared to $35,000,000 in 1921. This proved, the *Post-Dispatch* said, that conditions were not so bad after all.

But the *Post-Dispatch*, at the same time, was appealing to its subscribers to offer odd jobs to family heads so they could live without accepting charity. The city administration was making plans for soup kitchens and bread lines. The advance guard of an army of apple vendors was already on Houston's corners.

And Hobby's friend and colleague Ross Sterling was in deep trouble, in the Governor's Office and in his own business affairs. Almost from the day he was inaugurated, he faced one major crisis after another. One of the greatest was provided by the East Texas oil field, once hailed as the discovery that would make the state government depression-proof with its vast store of oil.

Instead its profligate production flooded the market, forced the price of oil down to ten cents a barrel, ruined the economy of the whole Texas oil industry—by now the state's greatest— and threatened to destroy its own rich reservoir. Proration laws were late in coming from the legislature and then were largely ignored. To save the Texas oil industry, Governor Sterling had declared martial law in the East Texas field.

It was the only course open, the *Post-Dispatch* kept telling its readers. With an assist from Congress in the passage of the Connally Hot Oil Act, Texas finally brought order out of chaos and went on to make history in oil and gas conservation. But Ross Sterling, forced into the role of pioneer in an originally unpopular area, suffered politically.

He was also suffering financially. On December 8, 1931, the banner line of the *Post-Dispatch* announced that J. E. Josey had purchased control of the newspaper from Governor Sterling. Loss of his newspaper was part of the price Ross Sterling paid for his whole-hearted devotion to state service.

Josey, a former Beaumont citizen and a wealthy insurance executive, announced that William P. Hobby would be in complete charge of the paper as president of the Houston Printing Company and publisher of the *Post-Dispatch*.

Hobby had virtually been in control while Sterling worked on the Highway Commission and then in the governor's job, but now the assignment was official. One of his first acts was to drop the hyphenated name and go back to the original name, the *Houston Post*. He had never liked the double designation but had said nothing in deference to Sterling's wish to carry on the name of his *Dispatch*.

Another early act was less to Hobby's liking. He had to go to the departmental staffs of the *Post* and reluctantly advise them that there had to be a stiff cutback in personnel. All staffs would have to work short-handed. The *Post* was fighting for survival, and it could win out only with the whole-hearted co-operation of all concerned. When Hobby finished his separate meetings with the various departments, an atmosphere of understanding had been created which enabled him to make the best of an unhappy situation.

Oveta had the leading role in the Hobby's next important production. She had been elected state president of the League of Women Voters, late in 1931, but even that honor was forgotten on Oveta's birthday, January 19, 1932. The evening papers scooped the *Post* with the announcement that William Pettus Hobby, Jr., had been born in Hermann Hospital at 8:20 A.M.

William was a healthy eight-and-a-half pound heir, and Governor Hobby enjoyed all the plaudits and prerogatives of proud fatherhood. "I had no idea babies were so popular," he happily confessed to Mrs. Hobby, "or I would have had them in my platform."

The new *Post* was not long in entering another political campaign. In fact, Will Hobby had about four campaigns going at once. He was actively backing Sterling's highway bond amendment, both as a constructive step for the state highway system and as "pump priming" to alleviate unemployment. The *Post* was also supporting Ross Sterling for re-election as governor, and booming John Nance Garner for president. And Hobby was a moving spirit behind a proposed plank in the Texas Democratic Party platform to refer the 18th Amendment to the voters for repeal.

Hobby, the lifelong antiprohibitionist who helped dry up Texas during World War I, now was an open advocate of repeal. He urged that the liquor question be brought before the National Convention. In 1918 the people had wanted prohibition; now they were fed up with a law that couldn't be enforced. Under the conditions, it might be better if a man could take a drink legally.

Hobby's idea for a prohibition referendum was overwhelmingly popular. Jim Ferguson became one of its strong advocates. Precinct, county and state conventions adopted resolutions calling for a national vote on repeal. Even such staunch dry's as Dan Moody and William G. McAdoo spoke out for resubmission.

An odd dispute arose between Governor Sterling and Hobby, his strongest supporter, over the prohibition referendum. Sterling first stated that the referendum had no part in the gubernatorial campaign; then he actually attacked it as having no place in a party convention. In spite of the Governor's opposition the state convention went for resubmission. On top of that, at Hobby's instigation, the State Democratic Executive Committee put the question on the primary ballot for a direct expression from the people to guide Texas members of Congress.

In July the Democrats nominated Franklin D. Roosevelt for president, with Texas' candidate John Garner as his running mate. Times had changed since 1928; Texans no longer objected to a New Yorker who favored repeal.

Sterling's attitude toward the prohibition referendum did not dampen the Hobbys' enthusiasm for his candidacy. Oveta, who had lived with Sterling's sister Florence when she first moved to Houston, was probably the Governor's most ardent campaigner. Even a broken arm and broken ankle suffered in a riding accident did not stop her for more than a few days. She was soon back on the telephone, working on precinct lists, exhorting the voters to support Sterling.

Again the principal opponent was Mrs. Ferguson. Marcellus Foster's *Houston Chronicle* was beating the drums for

"Ma," and the *Post* was equally insistent upon Sterling's re-election. The first primary election brought a foreboding of defeat for the incumbent governor. He was in the run-off by a good margin, but Mrs. Ferguson led him by 106,000 votes.

The run-off was acrimonious and hard-fought. Sterling, despite the handicap of having served during a time of economic disaster that left the voters eager for almost any kind of change, made a real race of it. At the finish it was so close that for several days the winner was not known. Finally Mrs. Ferguson was counted "in" by some 3,300 votes.

Sterling demanded a recount and the State Executive Committee was favorable, but in the end it was a Ferguson victory by 3,798 votes out of over 950,000. The repeal proposal carried, giving the *Post* some consolation.

Sterling bolted to the Republican candidate, Orville Bullington, in the general election. The *Post* went along only to the extent of showing voters how they could split the ticket to vote for Bullington and still support the other Democratic nominees. The Republicans worked up considerable steam but Mrs. Ferguson defeated Bullington by 211,000 votes. George Butte was still the champion Republican runner-up in Texas.

At that the state's only women governor, in winning her second term after a six-year hiatus, ran far behind the Roosevelt-Garner ticket which showed a seven-to-one margin in Texas. After the election the *Post* said it was apparent that a substantial majority of the citizens favored Mrs. Ferguson and that "it behooves all citizens to rally to her support."

The *Post* also was solidly behind Roosevelt's early "New Deal" programs, including the National Recovery Act, the farm support plan and certain amendments to the antitrust laws. In August, 1933, Hobby announced that the *Post* had signed and would immediately place into effect the NRA agreement for newspapers which provided for a forty-hour work week and a minimum wage of thirty-five dollars.

Later in the same month Texans voted for repeal of the prohibition amendment, for legalized beer and for a $20,-

000,000 relief bond issue, all of which the *Post* had been advocating.

Oveta, who had been active in the Women's Organization for National Prohibition Repeal, now turned her attention to the drive to assure the success of the NRA. She was also the book page editor of the *Post*.

The *Post* circulation dive had reached its lowest point early in 1933. With the stimulus to business that came from the Roosevelt Administration's confident leadership, the trend turned upward and subscribers started coming back at the rate of 500 a month. Will Hobby and Jesse Jones, who had been reappointed a director of the Reconstruction Finance Corporation by President Roosevelt and elected chairman by the other trustees, spoke out in defense of the Administration's program, which was already under attack from some business groups. Hobby cooled off a bit on the New Deal, however, over proposed food and drug controls for the Department of Agriculture. The *Post* said that Rexford Guy Tugwell wanted to set himself up as a "czar" and referred to him as a brain truster.

The Hobbys were behind every movement they considered to be for the public good. The *Post* seldom failed to live up to Will Hobby's conception of its obligation to the readers: Give the facts on all issues in the news columns, and express the *Post's* opinion without pulling any punches on the editorial page.

20

They Bought the Post

THE DEATH of G. J. Palmer on March 5, 1934, cost Will Hobby another longtime friend and caused him to ponder upon the changes time had wrought in the Houston newspaper world since Palmer hired him on the old *Post* at eight dollars a week. At the time of his death Palmer was business manager of the *Chronicle*, now owned by Jesse Jones. The fiftieth anniversary edition of the *Post*, coming out a month later, paid appropriate tribute in a ninety-eight-page Golden Jubilee issue to Palmer and the other giants of its formative years.

They passed in review through memory-laden columns: Sydney Porter, the immortal O. Henry; William Cowper Brann, the iconoclast; Rienzi Johnston, the inimitable editorial pioneer of the *Post;* Marcellus E. Foster, still displaying his fiery genius as editor of the opposition Scripps-Howard *Press;* J. L. Watson, founder of the modern *Post* dynasty in 1896, and his son Roy; Colonel George Bailey, Ray Dudley, Ross Sterling and the rest.

One thing that did not change on the *Houston Post* was its interest in politics. The election year of 1934 found Hobby in the thick of another fight with the Fergusons, although neither Jim nor "Ma" was a candidate. The Fergusons threw their support behind C. C. McDonald. The *Post* went all out for James V. Allred, youthful and vigorous attorney general of Texas.

Allred led in the first primary and McDonald finished third, but the Fergusons were not through. Tom F. Hunter emerged as Allred's challenger in the run-off and also as another Ferguson color-bearer. Allred's lead had been only 56,000. It was obvious that the expected combination of McDonald and Hunter votes would give Allred trouble in the second primary. Oddly, all three of the leading candidates claimed the same home town, Wichita Falls.

Will and Oveta Hobby not only supported Allred in the *Post* but urged their newspaper friends throughout the state to do so. The second primary brought in Allred as the winner by 40,000 votes. It was the last real fling for "Fergusonism." Mrs. Ferguson tried for the governorship once more, in 1940, but finished fourth in a seven-candidate first primary race.

In May of 1935, Hobby and Jesse Jones paid a personal call on President Roosevelt in Washington. A few months later the occasion of the visit came to light with the announcement that $650,000 had been allotted for improvements and repairs to the San Jacinto Monument, which pierced the sky above the last battleground of Texas independence. Jesse Jones got the allotment.

The year 1936 brought evidences of economic recovery throughout the nation and encouraging figures in the circulation books of the *Houston Post*. Subscribers now numbered just a few hundred short of 80,000, in pleasing contrast with the 1933 low of 62,000. It was also the Texas Centennial year, and Will Hobby, who had enthusiastically supported plans and appropriations for the celebration, was kept busy with speeches and other appearances throughout the state.

March 2, Texas Independence Day, was appropriately selected for an important presentation ceremony at Huntsville. J. E. Josey, the *Post's* owner, had bought the old Steamboat House, in which Sam Houston died, and was giving it to the State of Texas for a museum. Hobby was master of ceremonies. Governors of three states were present: LaFollette of Wisconsin, McAlister of Houston's old state of Tennessee, and Allred of Texas. Hobby, eyeing the trio of state executives, observed that he had often had occasion to look over one governor and see three platforms, but here was a rare opportunity to look over one platform and see three governors.

President Roosevelt came to Texas in June to join in the tribute to Texas' 100th birthday. Mrs. Roosevelt visited Houston, and Oveta accompanied her on a yacht trip down the ship channel. Then the Hobbys joined Jesse Jones in Dallas, where they were members of the President's party at the official Centennial center.

The return trip to Houston on June 12, by private plane with Jones and his secretary, Joe Toomey, proved to be an even more memorable experience. A short distance south of Dallas the plane burst into flames and went into a controlled dive. Co-pilot Eugene Schacher rushed out of the forward cabin to prepare the passengers for an emergency landing. Then he hurried back to help Pilot Edward Hefley, battling to keep the burning plane under control.

The small single-engined craft went into a steep dive, miraculously leveled off as it hit the ground, skidded 150 yards and came to a twisting, jolting stop in the midst of a group of terrified cotton choppers as the motor fell out and flames shot from the cockpit. Fire quickly enveloped the entire plane. Four men and a women burst out of the blaze. But there had been six people aboard.

Schacher, realizing that Hefley was still inside, dashed back into the flames and rescued him. None of the passengers was seriously hurt. Both pilots went to the hospital with bad burns. Next day the gallant Schacher died, a few hours after the Hobbys visited his bedside to thank him and Hefley for saving their lives. Will Hobby, although merely shaken up, was a patient in the same hospital. That was the last trip the Hobbys would take together by plane.

On that same dramatic June 12, Jim Mapes, the man who had taken over Hobby's papers in Beaumont, died suddenly of a heart attack. He was buried while Hobby was still recuperating from the effects of the plane crash.

Texas politics were mild in 1936. Allred was re-elected easily, winning a first-primary nomination over Tom Hunter and three others.

Will Hobby was still "Governor" to his friends and employees, and this occasionally led to complications. One post-midnight hour in the middle thirties a big story broke. The night editor had standing instructions to call Hobby when there were major news developments, no matter what the hour. He told the operator to get "the Governor" on the telephone. In a few minutes she reported the call completed.

"Hello, Governor?" snapped the night editor, no doubt anxious to prove he was wide awake even though it was well past midnight.

"Yes?" came the sleepy reply.

The night editor identified himself and started reeling off the details. The voice on the other end of the line expressed some interest and a little surprise at being aroused from a sound sleep for a purely local Houston story. The editor was puzzled at this reaction.

"Isn't this Governor Hobby?" he inquired.

"No, this is Governor Allred in Austin," came the reply.

After the night editor had apologized as properly as he could in his state of shock, he called the telephone operator and said, "Listen, sister, when anybody around this office asks for the Governor, they mean Governor Hobby. As far as this newspaper is concerned, there is only one Governor."

In 1937, Oveta acquired the new title of assistant editor. She retained her title as editor of the book page; however, her interest was turning more and more to the study and interpretation of current events against a historical background. In January, the *Post* started a series of Sunday features by the new assistant editor on subjects of international significance. The first was on the Ottoman Empire; others followed on such subjects as Turkey's Western constitution, Britain's pact with Egypt, Afghanistan, the Greek constitution. The articles, well-written and thought-provoking, required many hours of laborious research.

Meanwhile, Mrs. Hobby took time off for another unique birthday observance. On January 19, 1937, precisely five years and twenty-five minutes after the birth of William Hobby, Jr., and at the same hospital, Jessica Oveta Hobby was born. She was the third Hobby to share the birthday of General Robert E. Lee, which is an official holiday in Texas. Judd Mortimer Lewis had a poem ready for the new arrival. Governor Hobby had to miss Allred's second inauguration.

Hobby was soon to find himself at odds with the man he had stoutly supported for attorney general and governor. The *Post* had promoted a Harris County tax remission bill to afford funds for flood control. The bill passed both houses of the legislature, but Governor Allred promptly vetoed it on the ground that he disapproved of tax remission as a matter of principle.

The senate passed the bill over his veto, 18-7. Allred marshaled his forces for an all-out fight in the house. Here matters stood on April 21, the 101st anniversary of the Battle of San Jacinto. Houstonians arranged for house members to attend the dedication of the San Jacinto Monument. If occasion offered a chance to drop a good word about the flood control bill, so much the better.

On the ancient San Jacinto battleground two veterans of Texas political wars sat down and broke bread together that day. Jim Ferguson and Will Hobby had not been political friends for twenty years, but they had retained mutual respect. Next morning the *Post* carried a picture of the two former governors and perennial adversaries as they enjoyed fried chicken and Gulf trout and chatted together about old times, places and faces.

The San Jacinto junket, although successful otherwise, did not overcome Governor Allred's grip on the house of representatives. The house upheld his veto of the Harris County tax remission bill with strength to spare. The *Post* bitterly commented on Allred's use of a "Big Stick" and his "political shenanigans." Houstonians were assured that the fight was not over.

(And it wasn't. Two years later the legislature passed the bill again and Governor W. Lee O'Daniel—whom the *Post* had not supported—signed it.)

The *Post* was also at odds with a former idol on the national scene. Will Hobby's warm support of the New Deal had cooled noticeably over the Agricultural Adjustment Act of 1935, but he was still friendly until F.D.R. came out with his "court-packing plan" in February of 1937. At first the *Post's* editorials about court reorganization were cautiously worded and merely hinted at the dangerous precedent involved while admitting a need for judicial reform. But as the weeks passed and the extent of the Roosevelt plan was revealed, Hobby's attitude became one of firm opposition.

The *Post* was delighted to report that Roosevelt himself had spiked rumors that he might be a third-term candidate. Vice-President John Nance Garner was obviously the man deserving of promotion to the presidency, said Hobby after he and Jesse Jones had visited at Garner's home in Uvalde.

Hobby's disaffection with the New Deal did not keep him from observing the amenities when federal bigwigs came to town. He was on the reception committee when Jim Farley visited Houston, and the *Post* carried an editorial titled "Welcome James A. Farley." The editorial contained more criticism of the Roosevelt Administration, however, than plaudits for Farley.

The President himself stopped off briefly in Houston after a Gulf fishing cruise, and Will Hobby went with Jesse Jones, Mayor Fonville and County Judge Roy Hofheinz to greet him.

The "Hobby team," as such, was increasingly involved in almost every community project. The former governor gave the team dignity, experience and well-seasoned wisdom; Oveta contributed ideas, initiative and charm. They were active in the formation of the Houston Symphony Orchestra, in fund-raising plans for the University of Houston and were on many other boards and committees. One of Oveta's appointments was to a State Committee for Human Security, which sought appropriations for support of the needy blind and dependent children. She was inspired by this experience to write a series of articles for the *Post* on community welfare, dealing specifically with health, child welfare, leisure-time problems, and the merging of social agencies. Another appointment was to the national advisory committee for women's participation in the New York World's Fair.

In late January of 1938 the Hobbys were in Washington. The *Post* reported that Oveta had a chat with President Roosevelt at the White House on January 25 and later visited with William Bankhead, Speaker of the House; Sam Rayburn of Texas, House majority leader; and the Texas Senators, Tom Connally and Morris Sheppard. In March the directors of the *Post* promoted Oveta to executive vice-president. From that time forward she would assume more responsibility for day-to-day operations, with Governor Hobby continuing to make policy and answer the ceaseless calls of the community. An example was his service in 1938 as chairman of the Houston Chamber of Commerce Highway Committee, which contributed to the approval of a straight-line highway between Houston and Dallas.

It was another election year and all of the candidates for governor were new to the race except dogged Tom Hunter. The *Post* was torn between two strong contenders, Ernest O. Thompson, the railroad commissioner who was credited with saving the oil industry from economic disaster, and William McGraw, the popular attorney general. While the Hobbys and others were trying to decide between these excellent gubernatorial prospects, a political unknown came along and ran off with the election.

W. Lee O'Daniel, previously prominent only as a flour merchant and dulcet-voiced radio announcer, received more votes than McGraw, Thompson, Hunter and nine other candidates combined. The impetus of that phenomenal victory was to carry O'Daniel through another governor's race and a special and regular election as United States Senator.

The *Post*, which had castigated O'Daniel for his "professional politician's" gambit in the primary, continued to be critical of his pet "transaction tax" proposal as governor. Will Hobby appreciated O'Daniel's signing the tax remission bill which Allred had vetoed, but he said a transaction tax was just a sales tax under an assumed name and he was against it.

Meanwhile, when former governor Allred moved to Houston as a newly-appointed federal judge, the Hobbys gave a reception for him at the Houston Country Club. It was a typical gesture for Hobby, who never held political grudges.

Fall of 1939 found disturbing headlines flaring across the *Post's* front page. Hitler's war in Europe, long feared, had begun. The world was not, after all, as Woodrow Wilson had hoped, safe for democracy.

In spite of this the Hobbys still had confidence in the future of their country, state and community. They demonstrated it in striking fashion. They bought the *Houston Post*.

21

Will's Colonel Hobby

WILL HOBBY had run the *Houston Post* for fifteen years, but it was different having the title and the feeling of ownership. Half a lifetime of dedication to a dream that first stirred vaguely in the mind of a big-eared country boy, watching copies of the *Post* roll off the press on his way to school, had turned the vision into reality—a reality that actually was better than the dream.

With the year 1940 Hobby's *Post* entered a new era. Its history and traditions, its editorial flavor and its place as an important community institution would remain. The *Post* would become more and more, however, a reflection of its owners, Will and Oveta Hobby.

Improvements during the first few months included a new addition to the plant, new presses, improvement in the newspaper's content and appearance, a more readable format, increased advertising rates and a virtual elimination of newsprint waste. The *Post* had definitely weathered the depression and now was girding for expansion in a highly competitive field.

Will's and Oveta's own political and economic philosophy became more dominant in *Post* editorials, as befitted the increased stature of the newspaper.

The *Post* in 1940 was flat-footedly opposed to a third term for President Roosevelt. The opposition was not so much due to the Hobbys' distaste for some of F.D.R.'s policies as it was their sincere belief that the two-term tradition was worth preserving. They did all they could to help the Republican nominee, Wendell Willkie, without actually endorsing him. But when the election was over and Roosevelt had become the United States' first third-term President, the *Post* was quick to come out in support of national unity and a program of preparedness.

"The President is offering the nation a leadership that its safety demands it accept and follow," said an editorial. "It is high time that the people with one accord join in supporting the President."

War was moving in from both the Pacific and the Atlantic. Leading citizens were being summoned to Washington to aid in the feverish preparedness campaign. Late in July the call came for Oveta Hobby to head the women's section of the War Department's Bureau of Public Relations. Will Hobby took up again the full burden of directing the *Post* for the period of Oveta's Washington service, which both hoped would be brief.

Pearl Harbor dispelled that fond hope. Five months later, on May 12, 1942, Washington announced the creation of the Women's Auxiliary Army Corps. A few days later Secretary of War Stimson commissioned Oveta Culp Hobby as a colonel and gave her the assignment of running the WAAC.

The ensuing years would bring Colonel Hobby high acclaim for her remarkable job of organizing the first women's army in American history. Back in Houston Governor Hobby carried on with a depleted staff, as enlistments and draft calls cut deeply into the *Post's* man power. There was no letdown, however, in the vigorous policies of the newspaper. Hobby had already been to Washington to appeal for tax relief for small businesses. He opposed the absurdity of gasoline rationing in Texas, where more fuel was being refined than could possibly be transported away. He pushed the *Post* into a campaign to pay for a new cruiser to replace the *Houston*, lost in battle. The goal was attained by the sale of $85,000,000 in bonds at a rally on December 22, 1942.

Will Hobby had been one of the great state governors of World War I. He knew how to go about the business of supporting a war on the home front. Scrap iron drives, defense bond drives, civil defense efforts—these and dozens of other projects had the *Post* behind them.

In addition Governor Hobby gave countless hours to service on the Alien Enemy Board, which had the dual responsibility of assuring fair play for innocent citizens of enemy countries who were mere luckless pawns of war and at the same time keeping an eye out for the rights and security of the United States. It was an unglamorous and largely thankless task which Hobby tackled in much the same spirit as he mulled over clemency petitions while he was governor. Someone had to do this work, and Hobby was willing.

As for countless others, family life for the Hobbys was catch-as-catch-can during the war years. William Jr., and Jessica divided their time between Houston and Washington. On one January 19 they received birthday greetings from their mother in Algiers via United Press.

Multiplied honors came to Oveta. She was awarded honorary degrees by several prominent colleges and universities. The President, cabinet members, congressional leaders, generals and outstanding civilians were high in their praises of her services. Every word of it was music to the Governor's ears. His pride in his wife's accomplishments was beyond measure.

In May, 1944, General Dwight D. Eisenhower reviewed the anniversary parade of the Hobby troops, now an actual part of the army under the name Women's Army Corps. He paid glowing tribute to the women in khaki and to their efficient leader, Colonel Oveta Culp Hobby. Some years later Colonel Hobby and her husband would proudly return the tribute to "Ike."

Hobby and the *Post* were resigned in 1944 to the almost foregone conclusion that Roosevelt would seek a fourth term. It would be best, Hobby agreed with most Texans, not to change presidents at that stage of the war. This did not mean that he had weakened in his opposition to New Dealism, and the *Post* staunchly supported a political movement in Texas that was, in some degree at least, anti-Roosevelt.

The May Democratic convention, held in the state capital at Austin, split along liberal-conservative lines over the question of an "uninstructed" or a "Roosevelt-instructed" delegation to the National Convention. The conservatives, predominantly anti-New Deal, stayed in the senate chamber and the liberals marched across the rotunda to the more commodious house chamber. Governor Coke Stevenson, in his office down the hall, smoked his pipe in characteristic silence, but it was understood that he favored the conservatives. Both groups elected delegates. The delegates from the senate convention and their supporters became identified as the "Texas Regulars," because they represented the "regular" convention. After considerable jousting in the press and courts, both delegations went to the National Convention at Chicago and both were seated, with the Texas votes divided evenly between them. The "Texas Regular fight" was a source of bitter division among Texas Democrats for years.

Roosevelt was renominated and re-elected, as expected, but with a Missouri Senator named Harry S. Truman as his running mate instead of Henry A. Wallace. While Hobby would not oppose Roosevelt at this time for fear of contributing to national disunity, he continued to express himself through *Post* editorials concerning the New Deal. One of these, concerning "the degeneration of the United States Supreme Court under New Deal domination," appeared in June, 1944. Titled "The Crumbling Rock of Justice," it criticized Roosevent's appointments to the Court, the undignified attacks of Court members upon one another, several of the Court's decisions, and the alleged political bent of a majority of the Court. The editorial concluded:

"These animosities, and the partisan political activities of the jurists, and their marked lack of lofty judicial dignity that should distinguish a Supreme Court justice, all suggest that the constitutional plan of three separate and independent divisions of government has gone into partial eclipse. The thoughtful citizen has ample grounds to wonder whether we do not now have only TWO independent divisions of government—executive and representative. And if we do, is it not in order to think of some measure to restore the safeguards which the writers of the Constitution sought to provide?

"In other words, since the selection of Supreme Court justices by the method of executive appointment has failed to produce the kind of men needed for this exalted, highly specialized and extremely important work, in this critical hour of our nation's history, isn't it time the people took the responsibility of choosing them into their own hands, through the elective process?

"It is a question whose answer might mean the weal or woe of the Republic."

Renewed criticisms of the high court in the fifties were to echo some of these comments, but Hobby in 1944 was speaking to the current situation. This East Texas son of a distinguished jurist knew and loved constitutional government. Any yielding for the sake of political expediency, as he termed some of the Court's acts, was not in accordance with the welfare of the people.

The *Post* was less genteel in its comments when the President replaced Jesse Jones and named Henry Wallace as Secretary of Commerce. "It is a pity," said the *Post*, "to replace a man of Mr. Jones's distinguished ability with a left-wing ne'er-do-well in this critical hour of the nation's history, when the Commerce Department and the RFC bid fair to be crucial factors in our economic life—especially as a mere political reward for Mr. Wallace's political support of the fourth-term ticket."

The *Post* continued to lose the steadfast veterans who had helped Hobby build it to its present eminence. Early in the war H. L. Millis, then editor of the editorial page, had died of a heart attack. Hobby named Ed Kilman, a seasoned political writer, to the vacancy. In 1945 two of Hobby's oldest friends died—J. E. Josey, last *Post*-associate with whom Hobby served, and Judd Mortimer Lewis. Arthur Laro became city editor; his assistant was Harry Johnston, Jr., grandson of the illustrious Rienzi.

The devastating war was drawing to a victorious close. After Germany surrendered, Colonel Oveta Culp Hobby felt that her assigned mission had been accomplished. In January she had been awarded the army's highest noncombat decoration, the Distinguished Service Medal. She was the first woman ever to be so honored.

Three weeks after V-E Day, on May 27, 1945, Colonel Hobby took WAC salutes from a reviewing stand in Times Square, New York. On July 13 she asked to be relieved of active duty to return to her household and the *Houston Post*.

Houston welcomed Oveta back with a rousing flourish. At a dinner in her honor, with Mrs. Arthur Vandervoort as toastmaster, telegrams of praise and congratulation were read from President Truman, General Marshall, General Eisenhower and dozens of other national leaders. Significant, too, was the acclaim for Will Hobby. At the first mention of his name the 700 diners rose in a spontaneous ovation. When Oveta referred to Governor as "my partner, my friend, my husband," there was thunderous applause. The partnership of Hobby and Hobby was back in business.

Three days after Oveta left the WAC, history was made on the white sands of Alamogordo, New Mexico. There the first atomic bomb was exploded. Within a month Hiroshima and Nagasaki had been shattered by the terrible new weapon, and in a few days the war was all over. The *Post* supported with enthusiasm the prospect of a United Nations organization. In March, 1946, Mrs. Hobby told the National Council of Jewish Women's convention in Houston that the United Nations "must be implemented with an international bill of rights." She warned of Russian treachery in these words: "Shall we now insist that one of our former allies observe its agreement with Manchuria? Observe its agreement with Iran? Or shall we make a timid bid for peace in our time? . . . Does Russia think that we have not learned that small aggressions lead to larger ones?"

Later in March, Oveta covered the UN Security Council meetings in New York and wrote that it was "something like watching a chess game between powerful antagonists."

The year 1947 brought a major shuffle in the Hobbys' upper-echelon forces. Kern Tips resigned as manager of the *Post's* radio station, KPRC, to enter an advertising agency, and was replaced by Jack Harris, formerly a colonel on MacArthur's staff. Lloyd Gregory, former sports editor and managing editor, became vice-president and general manager of the *Post,* and the veteran Charlie Maes was promoted to assistant to the president. Arthur Laro took Gregory's place as managing editor and Harry Johnston moved up a notch to city editor. Some time later Gregory went into the advertising agency business and was succeeded by W. Howard Baldwin. Maes left the *Post* to join the Glenn McCarthy group of neighborhood newspapers.

There were other changes, also. Harry Johnston resigned as city editor in 1954 to join the Washington bureau of Time, Inc., being succeeded by Ralph S. O'Leary, an experienced newsman who had distinguished himself as a reporter on New Orleans and Saint Louis newspapers before coming to Houston. In 1950 Laro and Harris became directors of the *Post,* and in 1954 Laro was named executive editor, with W. D. Bedell as his assistant and Edward S. Welty as news executive.

Oveta Hobby became the first woman to be elected a director of the American Society of Newspaper Editors. She also received appointments to the United Nations Conference on Freedom of Information and the Hoover Commission on governmental reorganization.

Politics in 1948 gave the Hobbys pause on the national front. Governor Beauford Jester, who had defeated the deposed University of Texas president Homer Price Rainey in an explosive 1946 campaign, was re-elected without major opposition. But the *Post* could not work up any enthusiasm for any of the candidates for president.

Some months before, Hobby had been toastmaster at a dinner given by Hugh Roy Cullen and H. J. Porter at which Joe Martin, Republican Speaker of the House, was the honor guest. If any took this as a sign that a lifelong Democrat was going over to the Republicans, Hobby soon dispelled the impression. He faced the same dilemma of a great many Southern Democrats—dissatisfied with Truman as a candidate but still clinging to the Democratic Party.

The *Post* gave some encouragement to the States Rights Party, which had South Carolina's Governor Strom Thurmond as a candidate, and went so far as to suggest that a special session of the legislature be called to refer the States Rights issue to the people. Governor Jester declined to call a session, and the *Post* never got around to coming out for Thurmond. It did lean away from Truman, however, and suggested in a front page editorial that Texas' offshore oil lands —commonly called tidelands—were in danger of being lost, and that the Republicans could save them. Truman was elected, anyway, making the usual Democratic sweep of Texas votes.

As Oveta was being elected to the presidency of the Southern Newspaper Publishers Association, Governor was busy presiding over meetings of the Houston Chamber of Commerce Highway Committee, speaking at the laying of the cornerstone for the Ezekiel Cullen Building at the University of Houston, turning the first shovel of dirt for the Baytown-La Porte tunnel, which he had long advocated, and making the main address at a dinner for Bill Blanton, retiring manager of the Chamber of Commerce. At this last function Hobby introduced Sam Rayburn, thus squaring accounts with the Democrats for his participation in the Martin dinner.

High honors came to the *Post* in 1949, with four first places for editorial excellence in the annual Associated Press competition. The Hobbys felt that their newspaper was living up to its slogan, "Written and Edited to Merit Your Confidence."

Hobby and the *Post* had been among the first newspaper organizations to go into radio; now he and Oveta, who negotiated the deal, made another major step into a newer mass communications field by purchasing Houston's only television station. To promote Station KPRC-TV there were no crystal receiving sets to be given away with subscriptions, but a giant television show was staged on South Main Street at which the twenty-fifth anniversary of KPRC-radio was celebrated simultaneuosly. One of the features was the appearance of Governor Hobby and his first radio announcer, Alfred Daniels, on a special telecast.

Houston was growing and expanding at a rate that almost staggered the imagination. Governor Hobby was master of ceremonies as the Prudential Life Insurance Company broke ground for its new skyscraper, across South Main from the fabulous Shamrock Hotel. He commented: "Houston has reached the point where a ground-breaking has to be mighty unusual to get any attention at all. All we ask any more is 'Who's digging the hole?' "

22

Apples of Gold

THE LAST NIGHT of February, 1951, in the lavish Emerald Room of the Shamrock, was the occasion of the annual National Conference of Christians and Jews dinner in Houston. The honor guests were Oveta and Will Hobby.

Among the speakers was one of Will's oldest friends, W. Emmett Sampson. All the speeches were full of praise for the honorees, and Sampson's was no exception, but two of his comments about Will Hobby were especially significant. He spoke first of Hobby's great tolerance, which in this case was synonymous with brotherly love, the theme of the meeting. Then he spoke of Will Hobby's understanding sympathy for youth.

"His words of wisdom have calmed the souls and laid the path to many perturbed boys," Mr. Sampson said. "This spirit of helpfulness always reminds me of the beautiful words of King Solomon in Proverbs: 'Words aptly spoken are like apples of gold in a pattern of silver.' "

John L. Sullivan, former Secretary of the Navy, spoke of the principles for which the Hobbys stand and called them "effective Americans."

Governor Allan Shivers referred to Will and Oveta as "the real Mr. and Mrs. Texas."

"If I may speak personally," he said, "I feel that I have been strengthened, as a citizen and as a public official, by my association with them. I feel that I am a better man for having known them—just as the City of Houston, the State of Texas and this great nation of ours are better places because they passed this way."

As the evening wore on and the Hobbys listened to a dozen laudatory speeches, friends who knew Will best noticed a familiar merry twinkle in his eyes. They wondered how he would respond to the praise, recognizing all the while that he was deeply touched at sharing this honor with Oveta.

When his turn finally came, in the climactic address of the evening, Governor began: "Not only the spiritual element has been stimulating and inspiring, but I like the exaggerations, too—and 'exaggerations' is putting it mildly. Frankly, I feel like Groucho Marx who, after receiving a flattering presentation, said, 'After hearing that introduction, I can hardly wait to hear what I am going to say.' "

Then Hobby expressed his hope for better understanding between the religions and races of the world, which could come by applying the principles of the Lord's Prayer and the Sermon on the Mount.

Oveta had expressed a similar view: "The rule of thumb is a simple one. Regard each man, each woman, as an individual, not as a Catholic, a Protestant or a Jew; not as an Indian, American or European. Like or dislike a person for his own intrinsic qualities—not because he belongs to a different race or subscribes to a different religion. Dignify man with individuality."

She might have been describing Will Hobby's own attitude toward his fellow man. Protestant himself, a steward in the Methodist Church, he never made his own religion a standard for others to observe. As a matter of fact, Will Hobby liked nearly everyone, and nearly everyone liked him. When the storms came, as inevitably they did, his philosophy was simple. "Sometimes," he once told an assistant, "you just have to tie things down and let 'er blow."

The highlight of the evening for Will, an event which touched him even more than the warm words of his friends, came when young William stepped up to the platform and presented an orchid to his mother.

With that occasion remaining a pleasant memory, the Hobbys went back to the workaday world of newspaper publishing and community service. Sooner or later for Will Hobby, the trail always led back to politics. He was already deeply concerned, in 1951, over the presidential election of the following year. It was clear to him that Texas was rapidly approaching a political crossroads.

The major issue of '52, as far as Texas was concerned, would surely be the state's claim to the submerged lands in the Gulf of Mexico, out to the historical boundary of three marine leagues. This was the so-called tidelands issue.

Texas had claimed this underwater area at least since 1848, when the Treaty of Guadalupe Hidalgo, between the United States and Mexico, specifically set out the three-league boundary. The claim was never questioned until it appeared that there might be rich oil deposits under the offshore waters of Texas. Then a Supreme Court decision in the California tidelands case, speaking of the federal government's "paramount rights" in the offshore zone, clouded the Texas title. Members of Congress from California, Texas and Louisiana started clamoring for clarifying legislation, and got it—but President Truman vetoed the bill.

In the meantime all leasing, exploration and drilling off the Texas Gulf Coast came to a halt. No oil company could afford to drill on property without a clear title.

Hobby felt so strongly about the tidelands "grab" that he had virtually endorsed the Republican Tom Dewey in 1948 because of Truman's attitude. (Oveta visited Tom Dewey in Dallas and got his promise to approve a tidelands quitclaim bill.) The issue was not alone, or even primarily, one of oil revenues; the fundamental issue was one of unwarranted and unconstitutional federal encroachment on state rights and the abrogation of a formal agreement with the State of Texas.

The name of Dwight David Eisenhower began to be mentioned in a new context. The great war leader, a native-born

Texan, was a potential candidate for the Republican nomination for president. In Houston Jack Porter was ignoring "Old Guard" sentiment for Senator Taft and assuring his followers that Eisenhower would be nominated and elected. The *Post* conducted a poll in January, 1952, and learned that its readers favored Eisenhower by a good majority.

Following a pay-your-poll-tax drive which produced a record-shattering 337,000 qualified voters in Harris County, the Hobbys and the *Post,* with Oveta actively in the campaign, swung behind Eisenhower in earnest. When the General resigned his SHAPE command and returned to the United States on June 1, any lingering doubt was eliminated. Eisenhower was a candidate, and the *Post* was with him all the way. One of the most important reasons was: "He is in favor of state ownership of the tidelands, and against the federal grab of the submerged oil reserves."

Senator Robert Taft visited Houston and plainly said he, too, was in favor of returning the tidelands to the states. Will Hobby respected Taft and treated him kindly in the *Post,* but his keen political judgment told him that Taft couldn't win and Eisenhower could. He never doubted Ike's political appeal. Oveta, of course, was equally sold on Eisenhower as a potential winner, and even more enthusiastic than her husband over Eisenhower as a prospective president.

The May conventions in Texas, both Democratic and Republican, hit new highs in public interest. Allan Shivers was running for re-election as governor, with the *Post's* endorsement, and plugging hard for an uninstructed delegation to the National Convention. Party "loyalists," as they called themselves, wanted to pledge all convention participants to the Democratic nominees. Shivers refused to commit himself in advance of the National Convention, and upon that issue the rival forces locked horns. The result was a victory for Shivers and his conservatives.

Even more spectacular was the triumph of "Eisenhower Republicans" over the Old Guard in the GOP conventions. Hundreds of enthusiastic Eisenhower supporters swarmed to precinct meetings where, in other years, a dozen Republicans would have been a throng. Through their control of the party machinery the Taft Republicans managed to "carry" the state convention, but Jack Porter led a contesting delegation to the Chicago convention. Upon presenting proof of their overwhelming victory in the precinct and county conventions, the Eisenhower Texans were seated. Actually, the necessity of making a contest reacted sharply in Eisenhower's favor. Senator Taft's cause suffered irreparable damage from the charges of high-handed "steam-roller" tactics against his Texas followers.

With Eisenhower nominated by the Republicans and Adlai Stevenson, former Governor of Illinois, by the Democrats, the tidelands issue swung sharply into focus in Texas. Governor Shivers called on Stevenson for an expression on the tidelands question, and the Democratic nominee said he would have to follow Truman's course and veto any legislation quitclaiming the offshore areas to the states. That brought two of the state's top Democratic officials into the Eisenhower camp—Shivers, the nominee for re-election as governor, and Attorney General Price Daniel, who had been nominated in the primary to succeed Tom Connally in the United States Senate.

Shivers and Daniel campaigned aggressively for the Republican nominees under the banner of "Texas Democrats for Eisenhower." The September State Democratic Convention, at Shivers' insistence, put Stevenson and Sparkman on the general election ticket in the Democratic column but urged all Texas Democrats to vote for Eisenhower and Nixon.

During the campaign months Oveta Hobby was a leader in the national Citizens for Eisenhower organization. She worked most of the time out of New York headquarters while Will took care of Eisenhower's support in the *Post* as well as the multitudinous day-to-day details of publishing a newspaper.

Hobby was enjoying himself hugely. It was doubtful if even his own campaign, or those that he and Rienzi Johnston planned together in his salad days, gave him as great a thrill as the Eisenhower drive.

For the first time in history both major candidates for president visited Texas. Eisenhower spoke in Houston in mid-October and the *Post* reported that more than 65,000 people heard him. He was introduced by Senator-elect Daniel. The next night in San Antonio he was introduced by Governor Shivers.

Later in the month, when Stevenson came to Houston, the *Post* carried a banner line of welcome, but featured a front-page reprint from the *U. S. News and World Report* by David Lawrence titled "The 20,915 Who Can't Vote on November 4." The pointed reference was to the Americans killed in the Korean "police action," the prolongation of which the *Post* had frequently blamed on Democratic blunders.

As one of the climactic punches of the "Democrats for Eisenhower" campaign, Will Hobby appeared with two other former Democratic governors, Dan Moody and Coke Stevenson, on a filmed and recorded TV-radio program with Governor Shivers as moderator.

Despite the unprecedented and combined efforts of Republicans and conservative Democrats, the Texas result was in doubt until the last. It was conceded that Stevenson's "secret weapon" in Texas was the "straight-ticket" Democratic tradition that had been broken only once in the state's history. Under the circumstances, Eisenhower's 130,000-vote margin on November 4 was considered a sensational victory. Three other Southern states, Tennessee, Florida and Virginia, joined Texas in the bolt to Eisenhower.

Before the year ended, President-elect Eisenhower had named Oveta Culp Hobby to the position of Federal Security Administrator. Congress, at the President's request, created a new executive department to replace the Federal Security Administration, and the President promptly appointed her as the first Secretary of Health, Education, and Welfare. This gave her cabinet status.

Will Hobby was in Washington to escort his lovely lady to

the inaugural festivities. Then he returned to Houston and the familiar role of publishing the *Post* and keeping up with community projects for the Hobby "team" that once again, had been temporarily separated by a call to higher duties.

Hobby occupied himself with the opening of a new television center for Channel 2, the NBC outlet of his KPRC-TV station; with seeing young William through his final months at Rice Institute, guiding him into the position of assistant secretary-treasurer of the *Post*, and then bidding him good-by when he left for Navy service.

He and Oveta turned their attention to plans for a great new home for the *Post*. It would be one of the most modern newspaper plants in the country, and one of the largest in the South. He went to Washington as often as he could, and sometimes Oveta would slip away for unannounced visits back home.

When a newspaper feature described Oveta as the most important woman in the country, a magazine reporter asked Hobby for a comment.

"Well, I've known that for many years," he replied, "and I knew that some day the rest of the country would find it out."

Local and state politics absorbed Will Hobby's interest, as usual, in 1954. It became apparent that Allan Shivers would seek an unprecedented third term as governor. There was some speculation as to whether Hobby—a strong two-term advocate—would support him. One day Hobby picked up the telephone and called Governor Shivers in Austin. The conversation was brief, going something like this: "Allan, this is Hobby. I hear you are going to run for a third term. I think it is a good idea."

Shivers thanked him. In a few days he formally announced for another term. The *Post* gave him stalwart backing in a bitter two-primary battle with Ralph Yarborough, an Austin attorney whom Shivers had defeated in '52. Shivers won by some 90,000 votes.

Construction of the new *Post* building was now well under

way, with Governor Hobby almost literally counting the bricks as the walls went up. It would be the *Post's* fifth home. The plant built by Ross Sterling thirty years earier was obsolete. The new building was directly across Dowling Street from the old on a solid square block fronting on Polk Avenue. It was built in the shape of a giant T, with a 250-foot front. The center section carried the name of the paper and the words "Let Facts Be Submitted to a Candid World." The motto, of course, was adopted from the Declaration of Independence.

Before the new doors could be opened, Will and Oveta celebrated another event of vast personal importance. Young William Hobby was married to a lovely North Carolina girl, Diana Poteat Stallings. As soon as the wedding was over, Governor was back in Houston directing the placing of final touches on the *Post's* new home.

A more or less historic day was the period between the final *Post* edition of October 10, 1954, and the first edition of October 11. Between those editions a complete changeover of the mechanical department was made, and on the morning of the eleventh the first *Post* printed in a Hobby-built *Post* plant was delivered to some 200,000 subscribers.

The new plant had giant new presses mounted on separate foundations with a two-inch cork cushion, separating these foundations like a huge gasket to eliminate vibration, an age-old curse of newspaper publishing. It was completely air-conditioned and equipped with elevators, although it was only two stories high in front and three in the rear. Its huge editorial rooms included special offices for a modern newspaper "morgue" and library, for the women's page editors, sports editors, photographers, editorial writers, wire services and managing editor. There were handsomely furnished executive offices and spacious quarters for all department heads.

Will Hobby might well be called the father of special editions. He had pulled the *Beaumont Enterprise* out of financial straits with several well-timed, ad-filled special editions, and he had continued the practice at Houston. It was inevitable, then, that the formal opening of the new *Houston Post* building in January of 1955 would be observed with one of the most elaborate special editions ever published.

Titled "This Is Texas," the gigantic 302-page issue was divided into a dozen sections on such subjects as "The Government," "The *Post*," "The Land," "The Homes," "The Fashion," "The People," "The Resources," and "The Churches." The best writing talent in the state was tapped for special features. By-lines of noted Texas writers—Stanley Walker, J. Frank Dobie, Fred Gipson, Walter Prescott Webb, to name a few—were sprinkled liberally through the thick edition. The excellent writers of the *Post's* own staff outdid themselves. Printed entirely on Texas newsprint from the Southland Paper Mills at Herty, near Lufkin, which he had helped to promote in earlier days, the great edition was the crowning achievement of Will Hobby's long publishing career.

The pressures of single-handed executive responsibility, construction problems, the plant opening and the big edition finally caught up with Will Hobby and he fell ill. In August of 1955 Oveta resigned her cabinet position and returned to Houston to be with him. Her presence acted as a tonic for Hobby. Soon he was back on his feet and in the swing of Houston's mighty rhythm.

The masthead of the *Post* was changed again, with Will Hobby becoming chairman of the board and Oveta moving up as president and editor. Once more the Hobby team was functioning, full speed ahead.

On March 26, 1956, Will Hobby observed his seventy-eighth birthday, but he was too busy to do much celebrating. Another red-hot political year was in the making, and Hobby responded as the proverbial firehorse to the clanging of the fire-engine bell.

The Hobbys, rather naturally, wanted first to see President Eisenhower re-elected. Almost as eagerly, they wanted to see him carry Texas again. The prospect, offhand, was not encouraging.

The temper of Texas Democrats seemed to presage a sweeping return to their traditional support of the Democratic nominees. A test was provided in the May party conventions. Governor Shivers, going out of office, tangled with U. S. Senator Lyndon Johnson and Speaker Sam Rayburn—both staunch party men—over the leadership of the Texas delegation to the National Convention and took a severe licking. This was interpreted in most quarters as a portent of an easy Democratic victory in November.

The *Post* supported Shivers in the May conventions, then backed Senator Price Daniel in a more successful but still uncomfortably close victory for governor over Ralph Yarborough. These preliminaries behind them, the Hobbys were ready for the main event.

Again the contestants were Eisenhower, Republican and Stevenson, Democrat. Again Oveta was a leading spirit in the drive to enlist Democratic and independent voters in Eisenhower's cause, although this time she stayed in Texas and participated actively in the revived "Texas Democrats for Eisenhower" movement.

In 1956 the Democratic machine made a considerably more determined stand in Texas than it had in 1952. Some of the fervor was gone from the Eisenhower crusade, particularly among oil men who deplored his veto of a bill that would have removed natural gas production from any question of federal control. (Half-forgotten was his support of the tidelands bill; as in the old political joke, he "hadn't done anything for them lately.") Governor Shivers again stumped the state for Ike but the pundits calculated, on the basis of his defeat by Johnson in May, that his former vast influence had been dissipated by the attrition of long tenure in office and innumerable clashes with the "loyal Democrats."

When the returns came in showing that President Eisenhower not only had been easily returned to office but had carried Texas by an even greater margin than in 1952, just about everyone in Texas was surprised. Everyone, that is, except Will Hobby.

That canny, battle-seasoned observer had been supremely confident all along, even when Oveta and other Eisenhower people were most despondent, that the election was going to come out just as it did. Will Hobby had always had his finger on the pulse of the Texas electorate. He still did.

Oveta admitted she would have breathed easier if she had remembered the words of Adrian Pool, a former state representative from El Paso, who in years past habitually called Will Hobby for an election prediction. Almost invariably Hobby called the turn. Finally Pool, almost exasperated by Will's apparent clairvoyance, had exclaimed, "I know how the State of Texas can save a lot of money. Just call off the elections and let Hobby guess 'em!"

Another March 26, this one dated 1957, found Governor celebrating another birthday, his seventy-ninth, in a relaxed and happy atmosphere. The *Post* was gaining in prominence and power as the days passed, and by September had become Texas' largest daily newspaper. Houston was still growing; as Oveta once remarked, it was going to be a real nice town if they ever got it finished. The family was well, happy and together, at last in the same city.

And after all, it was the family—Oveta, William, Diana, Jessica and Henry (in February, 1958, Jessica married Henry Edward Catto, Jr., of San Antonio)—that meant more to Will Hobby than all the honors a grateful community, state and nation had heaped upon him . . . much more than the prestige and profit that his publishing ventures had brought. He was, first and last, a family man.

Oveta could recall an incident many years in the past, when William, Jr., was a very small boy, that told where the Governor's heart lay. While Hobby was on a business trip to Dallas, the family home, which was being remodeled, caught fire and was virtually destroyed. In the early morning hours she reached Hobby on the telephone at his Dallas hotel.

"Governor," Oveta began, "I'm afraid I have some bad news for you."

"Are you all right?" asked Hobby.

"Yes."

"Is William all right?" (Jessica was born later.)

"Yes."

"Well, then," said Will Hobby, and she could almost see the smile-crinkles around his eyes, "you don't have any bad news for *me*."

The house? Forget it; they would build another one. Will Hobby: one faculty that distinguishes him: he knows what is important, and what isn't.

INDEX

Born in Abita Springs, Louisiana, and reared in Beaumont, Texas, JAMES A. CLARK has been a resident of Houston for many years. Only two days after his graduation from high school in 1927 he became sports editor of the *Galveston News;* later he was statehouse correspondent in Austin and columnist and correspondent in Washington, D.C. He has been editor of several leading Southwestern newspapers, and is the author of the column, "Tales of the Oil Country," in the *Houston Post.* He was director of publicity, public relations and advertising for the opening and the first year of Houston's Shamrock Hotel.

In 1952 Mr. Clark collaborated with Michael T. Halbouty in writing the story of the fabulous oil field, *Spindletop,* published by Random House. Now a public relations consultant in Houston, he is the author also of *Three Stars for the Colonel:* The Biography of Ernest O. Thompson, published by Random House in 1954.

WELDON HART was born and educated in Texas. He was for many years on the staff of the *Austin American-Statesman,* which he served as sports writer and editor, and later as chief of the Capitol Bureau. In 1948 he became press secretary to Governor Beauford H. Jester, and served in that capacity with Governor Allan Shivers at various times between 1949 and 1957.

During the 1952 and 1956 presidential campaigns Mr. Hart was State Director of Democrats for Eisenhower. He was chairman of the Texas Employment Commission from 1953 to 1956. He is now engaged in public relations work in Austin.